# THE FIRST WORLD WAR

## WITH IMPERIAL WAR MUSEUMS

SARAH WEBB

**HODDER**
EDUCATION
AN HACHETTE UK COMPANY

The Publishers would like to thank the following for permission to reproduce copyright material:

**Photo credits**

**p.4** *Top row l-r* © IWM (HU 93563), detail; © IWM (HU 96671), detail; © IWM (HU 93520); © IWM (WWC SUPP. 20/33), detail; © IWM (Q 68089), detail; *bottom row l-r* © IWM (HU 93389), detail; © IWM (Q 68298), detail; © IWM (Docs. 16954 09/32/1-14), detail; © IWM (Docs. 16954 09/32/1-14), detail; © IWM (Docs.7107), detail, **p.5** *t* © IWM (Q 71266), detail; *center row l-r* © IWM (HU 93410), detail; © IWM (Q 107169), detail; © IWM (Q 70010), detail; © IWM (HU 93404), detail; © PA Photos / TopFoto; *bottom row l-r* © IWM (Docs.6620), detail; © IWM (HU 93392), detail; © IWM (Q 68187), detail; © IWM (Q 71266), detail; © IWM (HU 93549), detail, **p.8** © IWM (HU 68408), detail, **p.10** © IWM (HU 81831), **p.12** *tl* © IWM (K 44699); *tr* © IWM (HU 93410); *b* © IWM (Q 70214),**p. 13** *l* © IWM (Q 70010), detail; *c* © IWM (Q 68089); *r* © IWM (HU 93563), detail, **p.14** *t* © PA Photos / TopFoto; *bl* © IWM (PST 5129); *br* © IWM (PST 12226), **p.15** © IWM (PST 2763), **p. 16** *t* © IWM (PST 13654); *b* © IWM (Q 51866), **p. 17** *t* © IWM (EPH 5245); *b* © IWM (HU 52451), **p. 19** © IWM (ORD 125), **p.20** *tl* © IWM (Docs. 16954 09/32/1-14), detail; *bl* © IWM (Docs. 16954 09/32/1-14), detail; *br* © IWM (FEQ 829), **p.21** © IWM (Q 4652), **p.22** © IWM (Q 64485), **p.23** *t* © IWM (COM 176); *c* © IWM (MUN 397); *b* © IWM (EQU 3812), **p.24** *t* © IWM (Q 71266), detail; *b* © IWM (HU 93404), detail, **p.25** *tl* © IWM (HU 93549), detail; *tr* © IWM (HU 93563), detail; *b* © IWM (Q 2981), detail, **p.26** © IWM (Art.IWM ART 324), **p.27** © IWM (Q 2486), **p.28** © Idealink Photography / Alamy, **p. 29** © Sadık Güleç/iStockphoto/ Thinkstock, **p.30** *t* © IWM (Q 68298), detail; *b* © IWM (HU 93410), detail, **p. 31** © IWM (Q 13325), **p.32** © IWM (Q 10681), **p.33** *t* © IWM (Q 71266), detail; *b* © IWM (FEQ 366), **p.34** *l* © IWM (EPH 4379); *r* © IWM (EPH 1338), **p.35** *l* © IWM (Docs. 16954 09/32/1-14), detail; *r* © IWM (Docs. 16954 09/32/1-14), detail, **p. 36** © IWM (Q 24191) , **p.37** © IWM (Q 4694), **p.38** *t* © IWM (PST 10836); *b* © IWM (EPH 9442), detail, **p.39** *t* © IWM (Q 107169), detail; © IWM (Q28315) *b* © IWM (Q 28390), **p.40** *t* © IWM (INS 7767), *b* © IWM (Q 30040) **p.41** © IWM (WWC SUPP. 20/33), **p. 42** © IWM (PST 4470), **p.44** © IWM (HU 93520), detail, **p. 45** © IWM (Art.IWM ART 2242), **p. 46** © IWM (Q 110881), **p. 48** © IWM (Q 60474), **p. 49** *t* © IWM (HU 93392), detail; *b* © IWM (Q 70731), **p. 50** © IWM (EPH 9453), detail, **p. 51** © IWM (Q 65858), **p. 52** *t* © IWM (PST 12195); *b* © IWM (Q 54539), **p. 53** © IWM (Q 11759), **p. 54** © IWM (Q 48222), **p.55** © Daily Express, **p.58** *t* "The Menin Gate at Midnight" by Will Longstaff © Australian War Memorial; *b* © Brian Harris/ Rex Features, **p.59** *tr* © (Art.IWM ART 518), *b* © IWM ( Q 31438), **p.60** *top row l-r* © IWM (HU 93563), detail; © IWM (HU 96671), detail; © IWM (WWC SUPP. 20/33), detail; *bottom row l-r* © IWM (Q70010), © IWM (HU 93549), detail; © IWM (Q 68187), detail, **p. 61** *top row l-r* © IWM (Docs. 16954 09/32/1-14), detail; © IWM (Docs. 16954 09/32/1-14), © IWM (Q 71266), detail; *center row l-r* © IWM (Q 68298), detail; © IWM (HU 93410), detail; © IWM (Q 68089), detail; *bottom row l-r* © IWM (docs.6620), detail; © IWM (HU 93404), © IWM (Docs.7107), detail; © IWM (HU 93389), detail, **p. 62** *top row l-r* © IWM (HU 93520), detail; © PA Photos / TopFoto; *center row l-r* © IWM (HU 93392), © IWM (Q 107169), © IWM (HU 93389); *bottom row* © IWM (Q 71266), detail

**Acknowledgements**

**pp.5, 24, 33**: George Coppard, from *With a machine-gun to Cambrai* (Cassell Military Hardbacks, 1999); **p.11**: Georg Alexander Muller, diary entry, August 1914, from Annika Mombauer, *Origins of the First World War: Diplomatic and Military Documents (Documents in Modern History)*(Manchester University Press, 2013); Von Moltke, diary entry, 26 July 1916, from Annika Mombauer, *Origins of the First World War: Diplomatic and Military Documents (Documents in Modern History)* (Manchester University Press, 2013); **p.15** Godfrey Buxton, from IWM Voices of the First World War, www.1914.org/podcasts/podcast-37-conscientious-objection; **p.19**: Hermann von Kuhl writing in 1920, from Terence Zuber, *Inventing the Schlieffen Plan: German War Planning 1871–1914* (Oxford University Press, 2002); **pp.20, 35**: Fred Sellers writing to Grace Malin, 15 October 1915, (IWM Documents.16954); **p.22**: J.R. Ackerley, from *My Father and Myself* (The Bodley Head, 1968); **p.27**: Douglas Haig writing to Joseph Joffre, 26 May 1916, from Gary Sheffield and John Bourne (editors), *Douglas Haig: War Diaries and Letters 1914–1918* (Phoenix, 2006); **p.30**: Mustafa Kemal, writing on 25 April 1915. quoted in Peter Hart, *Gallipoli* (Profile Books, 2011), reproduced by permission of the publisher; Sir Hugh Simpson-Baikie, writing in 1915, quoted in Peter Hart, *Gallipoli* (Profile Books, 2011), reproduced by permission of the publisher; **p.31**: Edward Mousley writing in March 1916, from Gutenberg Project, *http:www.gutenberg.org/ files/41213/41213-h/41213-h.htm*; **p.33**: Harry Roberts, interview after the war, from *http: www.spartacus.schoolnet.co.uk/FWWfoot.htm*; Graham Greenwell, letter to his mother after the war, from http: *www.spartacus.schoolnet.co.uk/FWWfoot.htm*; **p.37**: Ganga Dut writing in January 1917, quoted in David Omissi (editor), *Indian Voices*

*of the Great War: Soldiers' Letters, 1914–1918* (Palgrave Macmillan, 1999); Dudley Meneaud-Lissenburg, in May 1915, quoted in David Omissi (editor), *Indian Voices of the Great War: Soldiers' Letters, 1914-1918* (Palgrave Macmillan, 1999); **p.38**: John Reith, from *Wearing Spurs* (Hutchinson, 1966); Captain John Liddell, letter to his family in November 1914, (IWM Documents. 11126); **p.41**: Madeline Ida Bedford, 'Munition Wages' from *The Young Captain* (Erskine Macdonald Ltd, 1917); **p.42**: Joe Hollister, letter to his father, 19 March 1917, (IWM Documents. 7847); **p.46**: Rudolf Binding writing in Spring 1918, from *A Fatalist at War*, translated by Ian F.D.Morrow (1927; Houghton Mifflin, 1929); **p.47**: Elfriede Kuhr writing in 1918, translated by Peter Graves, quoted in Peter Englund, *The Beauty and the Sorrow: An Intimate History of the First World War* (Profile Books, 2011), reproduced by permission of the publisher; **p.49**: Melvin Krulewitch writing in November 1918, quoted in Max Arthur, *Forgotten Voices of the Great War* (Ebury Press, 2002), reproduced by permission of The Random House Group Limited; Erich Maria Remarque, from *All Quiet on the Western Front*, translated by A.W.Wheen (Little, Brown & Company, 1929); **p.50**: Reginald Haine, reactions to the Armistice, quoted in Max Arthur, *Forgotten Voices of the Great War* (Ebury Press in Association with the Imperial War Museum, 2002), reproduced by permission of The Random House Group Limited; Thomas Gowenlock, from *Soldiers of Darkness*, (Doubleday, Doran & Co, 1936), **p.58**: Siegfried Sassoon, 'Reconciliation' from *Collected Poems 1908–1956* (Faber & Faber, 1984), reproduced by permission of the Barbara Levy Literary Agency; **p.59** F. G. Meade, letter to the Imperial War Museum, from http:// archive.iwm.uk/upload/pdf/Activity_4_Families_in_War_and_Peace.pdf.

Thanks to the trustees of the Imperial War Museum for allowing access to private papers in the Documents and Sound section, Imperial War Museums.

Every effort has been made to trace all copyright holders, but if any have been inadvertently overlooked the Publishers will be pleased to make the necessary arrangements at the first opportunity.

Although every effort has been made to ensure that website addresses are correct at time of going to press, Hodder Education cannot be held responsible for the content of any website mentioned in this book. It is sometimes possible to find a relocated web page by typing in the address of the home page for a website in the URL window of your browser.

Hachette UK's policy is to use papers that are natural, renewable and recyclable products and made from wood grown in sustainable forests. The logging and manufacturing processes are expected to conform to the environmental regulations of the country of origin.

Orders: please contact Bookpoint Ltd, 130 Milton Park, Abingdon, Oxon OX14 4SB. Telephone: +44 (0)1235 827720. Fax: +44 (0)1235 400454. Lines are open 9.00a.m.–5.00p.m., Monday to Saturday, with a 24-hour message answering service. Visit our website at www.hoddereducation.co.uk

Published in association with Imperial War Museums
IWM.ORG.UK
With thanks to Paul Cornish, Charlie Keitch, Anthony Richards, Helena Stride, Nicolas Vanderpeet

© Sarah Webb 2014

First published in 2014 by
Hodder Education,
An Hachette UK Company
Carmelite House, 50 Victoria Embankment,
London EC4Y 0DZ

Impression number 10 9 8 7 6 5 4 3
Year 2018 2017 2016 2015

Cover photo © IWM (HU 96426), detail
Illustrations by Barking Dog
Typeset in Chaparral Pro 11/14pt, layouts by Lorraine Inglis Design
Printed in India
A catalogue record for this title is available from the British Library
ISBN 978 14718 00184

# CONTENTS

**1914**
Aug War begins
Aug Defence of the Realm Act (DORA) passed
Aug/Sept Battles of Tannenberg and Masurian Lakes on Eastern Front
Sept Trench warfare begins on Western Front

**1915**
Jan Poison gas first used
Apr Gallipoli campaign begins
Dec Siege of Kut begins
Munitions crisis

**1916**
Jan Conscription introduced
Feb Battle for Verdun begins
May Battle of Jutland
Jul Battle of the Somme begins

# WHO FOUGHT IN THE FIRST WORLD WAR?

Armed conflict first broke out between Austria–Hungary and Serbia in the summer of 1914 and within three weeks much of the world was at war. Germany and Austria–Hungary (sometimes referred to as the **Central Powers**) were allied against Britain, France and Russia (known as the **Allies**). Other countries joined later, including Turkey and Bulgaria for the Central Powers and Italy and the USA for the Allies.

The impact of the First World War was huge. It involved 32 countries and was the first truly 'world' war. More men were killed than in any previous European conflict while **civilians** lived with the hardships of war for over four years, and even became targets themselves. The death toll for troops in the **British Army** and **British Empire forces** was enormous; almost one in every ten soldiers were killed (almost 1 million), and over 2 million were wounded.

▲ A map showing where the British Empire troops came from (highlighted in red).

## Faces of the First World War

These are the faces of some people from Britain and the British Empire whose lives were transformed by the War. Not all of these people survived it. Throughout this book, you will get to know some of these people and hear their stories.

▼ **Source A** Faces from the First World War.

Lieutenant William Hamo Vernon.

Lieutenant Joshi.

Privates Theo and George Seabrook and their brother Lieutenant William Seabrook.

Lottie Meade, a munitions worker.

Captain William (Billy) Avery Bishop.

Lieutenant Arthur Douglas Dodgson and daughter.

Private Reginald Roy Inwood.

Captain Fred Sellers, engaged to Grace Malin.

Grace Malin, engaged to Captain Fred Sellers.

Private Gordon Colebrook.

**1917**
Feb British re-take Kut
Apr USA joins the War
Jul Battle of Passchendaele begins
Dec Armistice between Russia and Germany

**1918**
Feb Ration books introduced
Mar German Spring Offensive begins
Nov Armistice

**1919**
Treaty of Versailles

Many, but not all of these people were from Britain. Just over 5 million men from the United Kingdom served in the British Army during the War. A further 3 million troops were from the British Empire, serving with the British Empire forces. The British had the largest empire in the world in 1914. It had approximately 445 million people, which was about one quarter of the world's population. From the Empire, India contributed the largest number of troops, at 1.5 million, followed by Canada then Australia.

Most of these troops were volunteers. **Conscription** was only introduced in Britain and New Zealand in 1916 and in Canada in 1917, elsewhere in the Empire there was no conscription. The legal minimum age for overseas service was 19 years old, but some younger teenage boys lied about their age to enlist. Most volunteers were sent to Europe, mainly to northern France and Belgium. However, fighting took place throughout the world: in Europe, the Middle East, Africa and Asia.

## ACTIVITY

1. Look at the photographs on pages 4–5. Who do you think is the:
   - youngest soldier?
   - the eldest soldier?
2. Read George Coppard's Story.
   a) Why did George want to enlist in the Army?
   b) How was he able to enlist despite being underage?
3. List the countries mentioned on this spread that fought in the War and indicate for which side they fought.

### GEORGE COPPARD'S STORY

'In 1914 … Rumours of war broke out and I began to be interested in the [soldiers] tramping the streets in their big strong boots … Military bands blared out their martial music in the streets. This was too much for me to resist and … I knew I had to enlist straightaway.

… Towards the end of August I presented myself to the recruiting sergeant in Croydon. There was a steady stream of men, mostly working types, queuing up to enlist. The sergeant asked me my age [sixteen] and when told replied, 'Clear off son. Come back tomorrow when you're nineteen, eh?' So I turned up the next day and gave my age as nineteen … and holding up my right hand, swore to fight for King and Country.'

Private Ivor Evans.

Florence Farmborough, Red Cross nurse.

Corporal Leslie Wilton Andrew.

Private Gordon Etheridge.

Lieutenant Walter Tull.

Captain (Bernard) Paul Beanlands.

Second Lieutenant George Doman.

General Sir Charles Carmichael Munro.

Corporal George Coppard (seated).

Private William Cecil Tickle.

**1914**
Aug War begins
Aug Defence of the Realm Act (DORA) passed
Aug/Sept Battles of Tannenberg and Masurian Lakes on Eastern Front
Sept Trench warfare begins on Western Front

**1915**
Jan Poison gas first used
Apr Gallipoli campaign begins
Dec Siege of Kut begins
Munitions crisis

**1916**
Jan Conscription introduced
Feb Battle for Verdun begins
May Battle of Jutland
Jul Battle of the Somme begins

# WHY DID TENSIONS DEVELOP BETWEEN EUROPEAN COUNTRIES BEFORE 1914?

The causes of the First World War go back to growing tensions between Germany, Austria–Hungary, Russia, France and Britain in the decades before 1914. Tensions stemmed from the fact that most of these countries wanted to increase or maintain their power in Europe. At the time, a country's power was measured by its wealth, military strength and the size of its empire. As a result, competition developed to build up economic, military and imperial strength. This fuelled rivalries which worsened relations. Countries sought security by allying themselves with others, resulting in the creation of two rival alliance systems in Europe.

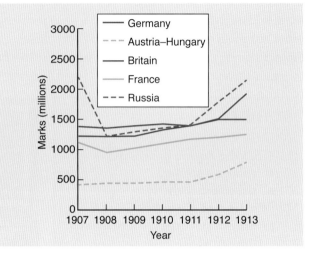

▲ The amount of money each country was spending on defence, 1907–13.

## Economic strength

The **industrial revolution** of the nineteenth century meant that the wealthiest countries were now those that could produce the most coal, iron and steel. Economic wealth and industrial output were both essential to building up military strength. Britain initially took the lead, but by 1910 Germany emerged as the leading industrial power in Europe.

## Military strength

Most countries in the decades before 1914 were keen to equip their armies with modern military equipment. They knew they would be at a disadvantage compared to their rivals if they did not. An **arms race** developed as countries spent more and more money on weapons. Germany was particularly alarmed by the sharp increase in Russian military spending (see graph above). Britain meanwhile interpreted German investment in their battlefleet as evidence of German ambitions to challenge the supremacy of the British Royal Navy. A fierce competition developed between them in building up numbers of **dreadnought** battleships. Some in Germany came to believe that if war was to come, they stood a better chance of winning if it was fought sooner rather than later before their rivals grew even stronger.

## Imperial strength

Competition for large empires was another cause of rivalry. Empires brought prestige and often increased economic strength as they were a source of resources and trade. Britain, and to a lesser extent France, had large overseas empires which they were keen to protect. Both were alarmed and affronted by the German Kaiser's aspirations to establish Germany as a world power. These common concerns helped to bring about an alliance between Britain and France who had formerly been rivals.

The Russian and Austro-Hungarian Empires competed for control of the **Balkans**. In 1908 Austria-Hungary added the Balkan territory of Bosnia-Herzegovina to its Empire. This angered Russia who became determined to resist any further extension of Austro-Hungarian influence in the Balkans. Austro-Hungarian control in the Balkans was also opposed by the Kingdom of Serbia who was keen to extend its own influence.

Both Russia and the Kingdom of Serbia supported the growth of Slavic **nationalism** which encouraged the **Slavic** peoples of the Balkans to resist foreign rule by Austria-Hungary. This contributed to unrest in the Balkans.

**1917**
Feb British re-take Kut
Apr USA joins the War
Jul Battle of Passchendaele begins
Dec Armistice between Russia and Germany

**1918**
Feb Ration books introduced
Mar German Spring Offensive begins
Nov Armistice

**1919**
Treaty of Versailles

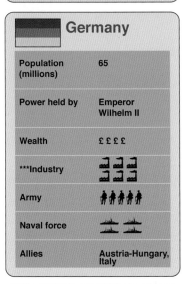

### Britain

| | |
|---|---|
| Population (millions) | 46 |
| Power held by | Parliamentary Democracy |
| Wealth | £ £ £ £ £ |
| *Industry | |
| Army | |
| Naval force | |
| Allies | France, Russia |

### Germany

| | |
|---|---|
| Population (millions) | 65 |
| Power held by | Emperor Wilhelm II |
| Wealth | £ £ £ £ |
| ***Industry | |
| Army | |
| Naval force | |
| Allies | Austria-Hungary, Italy |

### Austria–Hungary

| | |
|---|---|
| Population (millions) | 65 |
| Power held by | Emperor Franz Josef |
| Wealth | £ £ |
| Industry | |
| Army | |
| Naval force | |
| Allies | Germany, Italy |

### France

| | |
|---|---|
| Population (millions) | 40 |
| Power held by | Parliamentary Democracy |
| Wealth | £ £ £ |
| Industry | |
| Army | |
| Naval force | |
| Allies | Russia, Britain |

### Russia

| | |
|---|---|
| Population (millions) | 140 |
| Power held by | Emperor Nicholas II |
| Wealth | £ £ £ |
| **Industry | |
| Army | |
| Naval force | |
| Allies | France, Britain |

# Alliance systems

Countries made **alliances** to make them feel more secure. By 1907, two rival alliance systems had formed: the **Triple Alliance** (Germany, Austria–Hungary and Italy) and the **Triple Entente** (France, Russia and Britain). All alliance members, apart from Britain, promised to provide military help if their allies were attacked. Despite their defensive purpose, in some ways alliances actually increased insecurity because it seemed as if countries were forming threatening rival groups. Germany, in particular, felt surrounded by hostile countries.

## ACTIVITY

1. What does the graph on page 6 suggest about why there might have been growing tensions between European countries before 1914?
2. Look at the cards on this page showing the status of those European countries that went to war in 1914.
   a) List the strengths and weaknesses of each major European country around 1914 that went to war.
   b) What main worries do you think members of the Triple Entente had about the Triple Alliance?
   c) What main worries do you think members of the Triple Alliance had about the Triple Entente?
3. Tensions between countries were caused by economic developments, military and imperial strength and alliance systems.
   a) Draw a mind map with 'Reasons for tensions between countries' in the middle, giving examples for each main cause: economic strength, imperial strength, military strength, alliance systems.
   b) Draw arrows between the four main factors and add your own notes to show ways in which they were linked.

\* The leading producer until the early 1900s. Wanted to regain this position.
\*\* Still not much modern industry but output was increasing quickly.
\*\*\* Had recently become the leading industrial producer and output continued to increase.

Italy, a member of the Triple Alliance, did not actually go to war on the side of its allies Germany and Austria-Hungary in 1914. Italy joined the War in 1915, but on the side of the Triple Entente.

**1914**
Aug War begins
Aug Defence of the Realm Act (DORA) passed
Aug/Sept Battles of Tannenberg and Masurian Lakes on Eastern Front
Sept Trench warfare begins on Western Front

**1915**
Jan Poison gas first used
Apr Gallipoli campaign begins
Dec Siege of Kut begins
Munitions crisis

**1916**
Jan Conscription introduced
Feb Battle for Verdun begins
May Battle of Jutland
Jul Battle of the Somme begins

# DID COUNTRIES' MILITARY PLANS MAKE WAR MORE LIKELY?

Every major European country had drawn up military plans in the decades before 1914. These set out how their armies should act to give themselves the best chance of victory in the event of a war.

## German military plans

Germany was in a particularly vulnerable position if war did break out. This was because Germany would have to face a war on two fronts; against France to the west and against Russia to the east. The German Army was strong, but not strong enough to divide its strength and win.

The German military plan was based on the ideas of the German General Alfred von Schlieffen, drawn up in the 1890s. It became known as the Schlieffen Plan. It argued that the best hopes for a German victory lay in avoiding a two front war. It set out that this could be achieved by launching such a massive and rapid attack to the west that Belgium and France would be defeated within six weeks. It was estimated that the vast Russian Army would take eight weeks to mobilise and be ready for action. A full scale two front war could therefore be avoided because German troops would have already defeated France before having to face the full force of the Russian Army.

The key to the success of the plan was an invasion to the west that was swift and forceful enough to outmanoeuvre

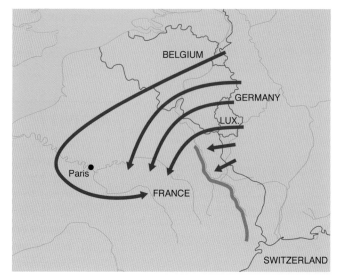

▲ The original Schlieffen Plan.

French and Belgian troops. To achieve this the plan said that over 1 million German troops would advance rapidly in a 'hook' like formation through the largely flat terrain of Belgium and northern France, thereby avoiding the strong French fortifications along the Franco-German border (see the purple line on the map above). It was a risky plan. To have any chance of success German troops would have to strike first before French and Belgian troops were prepared and ready for action.

**1917**
Feb British re-take Kut
Apr USA joins the War
Jul Battle of Passchendaele begins
Dec Armistice between Russia and Germany

**1918**
Feb Ration books introduced
Mar German Spring Offensive begins
Nov Armistice

**1919**
Treaty of Versailles

## Austro-Hungarian military plans

Austria-Hungary also had to face the threat of a war on multiple fronts, against the Kingdom of Serbia to the south and Russia to the east. The Austro-Hungarian Army was comparatively weak and as such wanted to avoid war unless help from its German ally was guaranteed.

## Russian military plans

The Russian Army was vast but under-resourced (see page 7). It took a large amount of time to organise its troops to be ready for action. Russian military plans emphasised that it was vital that the order be given to mobilise the Russian Army early, well in advance of the need to actually fight. However, an early mobilisation order would alarm other countries and might panic them into thinking that Russia was threatening war.

## French military plans

French military planners believed the best hope of achieving victory was by launching a large scale, rapid attack across the Franco-German border. The French were confident that the strong fortifications they had built along the Franco-German border would be sufficient to seriously protect against a German invasion.

## British military plans

The British had a relatively small professional army in 1914 (see page 7). They did not want to be involved in a large scale war in Europe. However, they planned to send troops to help France in the event of a German attack. This was because Britain was keen to prevent what they saw as the threat of German domination in Europe. British military planners believed that the British Royal Navy should be its biggest contribution, acting to destroy the German navy and **blockading** German ports to prevent the receipt of vital supplies.

◄ The Kaiser and his party watch proceedings on horseback during the manoeuvres of 1899. The Kaiser is turning round to laugh with General von Schlieffen, Chief of General Staff (fourth from right).

## Did military plans make war more likely?

In some ways the plans made war more likely. German leaders knew that Germany's best, perhaps only hope of survival, was if they were able to attack *before* they were attacked. This might make German leaders more likely to escalate to war rather than negotiate if a conflict seemed likely. Russia knew they had to mobilise early to stand a chance of victory. This might make Russian leaders more likely to order early mobilisation which would panic other countries into thinking war was imminent. All countries felt reasonably confident in their military plans. Might this mean they were more likely to risk involvement in a war? Despite these things, the military plans did not mean that countries wanted war. The plans were there to make sure their armies were best prepared if a war broke out. There was no immediate sign that it would at the beginning of 1914.

**ACTIVITY**
1. Why did German generals feel Germany's best hope of victory was by following the Schlieffen Plan? Try to identify three reasons.
2. Try to think of three risks which might cause the Schlieffen Plan to fail? Use the diagram on page 8 to help you.
3. How far, if at all, do you think the military plans made war more or less likely? Mark your view on the continuum below and give reasons to support your position.

**War less likely** ⟶ **War more likely**

**1914**
Aug War begins
Aug Defence of the Realm Act (DORA) passed
Aug/Sept Battles of Tannenberg and Masurian Lakes on Eastern Front
Sept Trench warfare begins on Western Front

**1915**
Jan Poison gas first used
Apr Gallipoli campaign begins
Dec Siege of Kut begins
Munitions crisis

**1916**
Jan Conscription introduced
Feb Battle for Verdun begins
May Battle of Jutland
Jul Battle of the Somme begins

# WHAT EVENTS LED TO THE OUTBREAK OF WAR IN THE SUMMER OF 1914?

Despite growing tensions in 1914, war did not seem immediately likely. Then, on 28 June 1914, a fatal double shooting in Austria–Hungary provided the trigger for war.

## The trigger

The victims of the **assassination** were Archduke Franz Ferdinand, the heir to the throne of Austria–Hungary, and his wife Sophie. They were killed in the city of Sarajevo in Bosnia, which had recently become part of Austria–Hungary (see page 6). The gunman was nineteen-year-old Gavrilo Princip. He belonged to Young Bosnia, a **terrorist** group committed to ending Austria–Hungary's control of Bosnia. Young Bosnia received weapons and funding from powerful Serbian individuals. Austria–Hungary was quick to blame Serbia for the assassination, partly because they had been looking for an opportunity to attack Serbia, one of their rivals for control in the Balkans.

## How did the assassination lead to war?

The events triggered by the assassination meant that within six weeks of the Archduke's death much of Europe was at war. The timeline opposite shows how events unfolded.

**Source A** Theobald Bethmann Hollweg, the German Chancellor (the leading German politician), speaking in August 1914.

Should all our attempts [for peace] be in vain … we shall go into the field of battle with a clear conscience and the knowledge that we did not desire this war.

▼ **Source B** Archduke Franz Ferdinand and his wife entering their car in Sarajevo, a few moments before the assassination on 28 June 1914.

| 1917 | 1918 | 1919 |
|------|------|------|
| Feb British re-take Kut | Feb Ration books introduced | Treaty of Versailles |
| Apr USA joins the War | Mar German Spring Offensive begins | |
| Jul Battle of Passchendaele begins | Nov Armistice | |
| Dec Armistice between Russia and Germany | | |

**28 June** The heir to the throne of Austria–Hungary is assassinated.

**5 July** Germany promised to support Austria–Hungary in taking action against Serbia.

**23 July** Austria–Hungary issued a harsh ultimatum to Serbia, threatening them with war unless all demands were agreed to.

**28 July** Austria–Hungary, encouraged and assured of support from its German ally, declared war on Serbia.

**29 July** Peace talks were suggested by Britain but never took place. Russia ordered its army to prepare for possible military action. Russia was desperate to prevent Austria–Hungary gaining further influence in the Balkans.

**30 July** Germany warned Russia to stop preparing its army. Russia refused.

**1 August** Germany declared war on Russia.

**3 August** Because of the Schlieffen Plan (see page 8), Germany declared war on France and invaded Belgium.

**4 August** Britain declared war on Germany, claiming they were honouring their 1839 promise to protect Belgium.

**6 August** Austria–Hungary declared war on Russia. Serbia declared war on Germany.

**12 August** Britain and France declared war on Austria–Hungary.

▲ The main events that led to the outbreak of war in 1914.

# Did countries want war in the summer of 1914?

Germany, Austria-Hungary and Russia all appeared to take aggressive actions in the lead up to the outbreak of war (see timeline). Did this mean that these countries had just been looking for an excuse to go to war? German and Russian leaders claimed they did not want war, as Sources A and C suggest. However, not all the evidence suggests that war was unwanted, whether this was because conflict was actually seen as the best means of defence or as an opportunity to preserve and extend power, see Sources D and E. Many countries ended up at war because they feared the consequences of not going to war *more* than they feared war itself.

**Source C** Extracts from telegrams sent between Tsar Nicholas II, ruler of Russia, and Kaiser Wilhelm II, ruler of Germany, on 28 July 1914. Nicholas II and Wilhelm II were cousins.

[To Kaiser Wilhelm II] To try and avoid such a calamity as a European war, I beg you in the name of our old friendship to do what you can to stop your allies from going too far. Nicky.

[To Tsar Nicholas II] With regard to the hearty and tender friendship which binds us both from long ago, I am exerting my utmost influence to arrive at a satisfactory understanding with you. Your sincere and devoted friend and cousin. Willy.

The war that broke out in the summer of 1914 was in some ways the anticipated result of tensions and rivalries that had been building up between countries for decades (see pages 6–7). But the rapid descent into war also took people by surprise; arguably even Europe's leaders had hoped to avoid actual hostilities in the summer of 1914. But recklessness, fear, ambition and miscalculation all contributed to the outbreak of war in the summer of 1914.

**Source D** Georg Alexander Müller, an admiral in the German navy and friend of the Kaiser, writing in his diary in August 1914.

Brilliant mood. The government has succeeded very well in making us appear as the attacked.

**Source E** Von Moltke, the leading general of the German Army, 26 July 1914.

We shall never again strike as well as we do now, with France's and Russia's expansion of their armies incomplete.

## ACTIVITY

1.  a) For each of the following countries, write down the actions they took which contributed to the outbreak of war: Austria–Hungary, Serbia, Germany, Russia, Britain.
    b) Rank these countries from most to least responsible for causing the War. Try to think about their motives as well as their actions. Explain your rankings.
2.  a) How far do Source A, C, D and E agree about German motives in the lead up to war?
    b) What motives might other countries have had for going to war?
3.  To what extent was the arms race responsible for the outbreak of war in 1914? Try to include all the reasons you have learned about in pages 6–11 in your answer. Your answers should explain your view about which reasons were most important or how they were linked together.

**1914**
Aug War begins
Aug Defence of the Realm Act (DORA) passed
Aug/Sept Battles of Tannenberg and Masurian Lakes on Eastern Fron
Sept Trench warfare begins on Western Front

**1915**
Jan Poison gas first used
Apr Gallipoli campaign begins
Dec Siege of Kut begins
Munitions crisis

**1916**
Jan Conscription introduced
Feb Battle for Verdun begins
May Battle of Jutland
Jul Battle of the Somme begins

# WHO WERE THE MEN WHO WENT TO WAR?

As soon as war broke out, the British government appealed for civilian volunteers to join the army. The government realised that Britain's army of around 700,000 troops would not be enough to win. The public response was enthusiastic. Within eight weeks 750,000 men had voluntarily enlisted. During the War this grew to a total of 2.67 million men.

Men from all social classes and backgrounds volunteered. The majority were young men. An initial upper age limit of 30 was set for volunteers with no previous military experience, although this was later slightly increased. The minimum age for military service overseas was nineteen, but with recruiting officers paid a bonus for each new recruit, some underage boys illicitily enlisted.

A MAN FROM THIS HOUSE

**NOT AT HOME**

NOW SERVING IN HIS MAJESTY'S FORCES

**IVOR'S STORY**
Ivor Evans was just fifteen when he joined up in August 1914. He was from a working class background in Swansea in Wales where his father worked as a lead smelter. Ivor served in Gallipoli (see page 28), Greece and France.

▼ **Source A** Sikh soldiers arriving in France as part of the British Empire forces (1914). A woman is pinning a flower onto the tunic of one of the soldiers.

▲ **Source B** A notice people could put in their window, showing their pride that a family member had volunteered to fight.

**1917**
Feb British re-take Kut
Apr USA joins the War
Jul Battle of Passchendaele begins
Dec Armistice between Russia and Germany

**1918**
Feb Ration books introduced
Mar German Spring Offensive begins
Nov Armistice

**1919**
Treaty of Versailles

# From volunteers to conscripts

When Britain declared war it meant that countries in the British Empire were also at war. Bt 1918 almost 30 per cent of men who fought for British forces in the War were from the British Empire (see page 4). As the War dragged on, fewer people volunteered to serve and the government felt it necessary to introduce conscription in Britain. Eventually 2.77 million British men were conscripted into the British Army.

### LESLIE'S STORY

From New Zealand, Leslie Wilton Andrew volunteered for the army at the age of eighteen in 1915, having previously worked as an administrator for a railway company. He travelled the long journey to France by boat, briefly stopping off in Egypt. In 1917 he was awarded the **Victoria Cross** for bravery in capturing a vital German machine gun during a battle.

### BILLY'S STORY

Billy (William) Avery Bishop, from Ontario in Canada, volunteered in 1914 at the age of twenty. The War seemed to offer an opportunity, as he was failing in his college studies. He was initially to serve in the **cavalry** since he was a good rider. The ocean crossing from Canada to England took fifteen days. He shared a boat with 700 seasick horses – a 'very unpleasant experience'. While at a training camp in England he saw an aeroplane from the Royal Flying Corps (RFC), which had only been established in 1912, and immediately wanted to become a pilot. He transferred to the RFC in 1915 and was given pilot training. He went on to become a highly successful pilot with the Royal Flying Corps; he claimed to have shot down 72 enemy aircraft. He was awarded the Victoria Cross in 1917.

### WILLIAM'S STORY

William Hamo Vernon was from a privileged background. His grandfather was a baronet and William attended Sedbergh School, a public school in Cumbria. William was one of over 1,200 former Sedbergh School pupils to volunteer, enlisting at the age of nineteen. Privileged, educated young men like William tended to become the young junior officers who would lead the new recruits into battle. Officers were a particular target in battle and suffered a higher death rate than other ranks. One in five Sedbergh pupils who volunteered would not return from the War.

### ACTIVITY

1. Use the information from the profiles on this page to record the following information:

| Name | Age enlisted | Background/occupation before enlisted | Nationality |
|------|------|------|------|
|  |  |  |  |

2. In what ways is the evidence in your table
   a) representative and
   b) not representative of men who fought for Britain and the British Empire during the War?

3. Think of reasons why each of the men featured on this page might have volunteered. Write a list. You will find out some of the reasons men enlisted on pages 14–17.

1914
Aug War begins
Aug Defence of the Realm Act (DORA) passed
Aug/Sept Battles of Tannenberg and Masurian Lakes on Eastern Front
Sept Trench warfare begins on Western Front

1915
Jan Poison gas first used
Apr Gallipoli campaign begins
Dec Siege of Kut begins
Munitions crisis

1916
Jan Conscription introduced
Feb Battle for Verdun begins
May Battle of Jutland
Jul Battle of the Somme begins

# WHY DID SOME MEN VOLUNTEER TO FIGHT AND OTHERS REFUSE TO FIGHT?

Men volunteered for lots of reasons. Some felt it was their duty. Others felt a sense of **patriotism** or saw it as an adventure, and some did not want to be labelled cowards. The British government set up the Parliamentary Recruiting Committee to encourage men to enlist. They produced 12.5 million recruitment posters during the War.

Some men were attracted by the promise that groups who enlisted together would stay together, in 'pals' battalions. Others were tempted by army pay and travel opportunities. Social pressures meant that men who did not want to fight were often made to feel humiliated and ashamed. Some women handed out white feathers, a symbol of cowardice, to young men they saw in civilian clothes rather than army uniforms.

**WALTER'S STORY**

Walter Tull was a professional footballer, playing for Tottenham and then Northampton Town, when war broke out in 1914. He volunteered to fight in the Footballer's Battalion, a special 'pals' battalion made up of professional footballers. He fought in France and Italy, showing bravery and skill which led to him being recommended for promotion. Walter became the first black officer in the British Army.

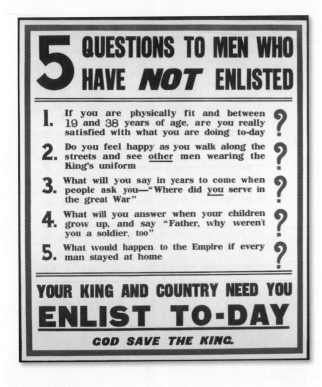

▲ **Source A** A British recruitment poster.

▲ **Source B** An Australian recruitment poster for a special 'pals' battalion of sportsmen.

1917
Feb British re-take Kut
Apr USA joins the War
Jul Battle of Passchendaele begins
Dec Armistice between Russia and Germany

1918
Feb Ration books introduced
Mar German Spring Offensive begins
Nov Armistice

1919
Treaty of Versailles

# Why did some men refuse to fight?

Exemptions from military service were available to some men, for example those engaged in work vital to the war effort or sole providers for families with children. In the first year of conscription, 80,000 men were exempted. These included men known as conscientious objectors who refused to fight on the grounds of conscience or religion. These were mostly pacifists, socialists or Quakers. Around 16,500 men, whose claims for exemption were disputed appeared before tribunals.

A military tribunal would assess the objector's claim. The majority were exempted or offered the opportunity of serving in a non-combative role, such as ambulance or transport drivers. But there were around 6,000 men who refused to take any part in the War, and were imprisoned. Conscientious objectors, 'conchies', were often portrayed as cowards who shirked their duty to fight while other men fought and died.

## Source D
Godfrey Buxton, a conscientious objector, describing reasons for refusing conscription.

'One met people who didn't quite know which way to go and some who felt very strongly for religious reasons – others for political reasons – that they wouldn't take part. I think really at that stage I was so young that I wasn't really thinking it through. There were some who were purely political conscientious objectors. But from the Christian point of view I think people took that phrase 'Thou Shalt not Kill'… [as] final to some people'

## ACTIVITY
1. Choose one of the posters on pages 14–15 and explain whether you think it was effective in appealing to men to join up. Give reasons for your answer by referring in detail to the poster.
2. a) Create a mind map with the title: 'Why did men volunteer for the army?' Use the text and the Sources to find as many reasons as you can.
   b) Can you group these reasons into categories? For example: patriotic reasons, social pressures, reasons to do with a sense of duty.
3. a) How were conscientious objectors treated during the War?
   b) Why do you think they were treated in these ways?

◀ **Source C** A British recruitment poster (1915).

**1914**
Aug War begins
Aug Defence of the Realm Act (DORA) passed
Aug/Sept Battles of Tannenberg and Masurian Lakes on Eastern Front
Sept Trench warfare begins on Western Front

**1915**
Jan Poison gas first used
Apr Gallipoli campaign begins
Dec Siege of Kut begins
Munitions crisis

**1916**
Jan Conscription introduced
Feb Battle for Verdun begins
May Battle of Jutland
Jul Battle of the Somme begins

# DID ANTI-GERMAN PROPAGANDA CAUSE PEOPLE TO ENLIST?

The media produced a lot of anti-German propaganda to persuade men to enlist. It promoted the view that it was right and necessary to fight against Germany, which was shown as a devious, savage aggressor.

During the invasion of Belgium and France in 1914, the German Army was responsible for the deaths of over 5,000 Belgian civilians. The British press reported these crimes and soon stories of German atrocities against civilians became wildly exaggerated. The sinking of the British cruise liner the *Lusitania* on 7 May 1915 added to the hate against Germany. The ship had been *en route* between New York and Liverpool when it was sunk by a torpedo fired from a German **U-boat**, causing the deaths of 1,198 of the passengers. The deaths included people from Britain and the USA, and over 300 women and children.

The British press presented the sinking as a callous, unjustified attack on civilians, and there were anti-German riots in Britain and the USA. The truth was more complicated. Germany justified the sinking by arguing that the *Lusitania* was carrying a secret cargo of weapons from the USA to Britain.

**Source A** An Irish recruitment poster produced ▶ after the sinking of the *Lusitania* in May 1915.

## *LUSITANIA* MEDAL

This medal was first produced by a German company to commemorate the sinking of the *Lusitania*. It shows the *Lusitania* sinking, with guns and aircraft on the decks. The caption reads: 'No contraband (banned goods). The large steamer the *Lusitania* sunk by a German submarine, 7 May 1915.'

The medal was then reproduced in England, as anti-German propaganda, to show how Germany was cruelly celebrating the sinking. A propaganda flyer printed with the reproduced medals included the statement: 'The designer has put in guns and aeroplanes, which the *Lusitania* did not carry, but has conveniently omitted to put in the women and children, which the world knows she did carry.'

**1917**
Feb British re-take Kut
Apr USA joins the War
Jul Battle of Passchendaele begins
Dec Armistice between Russia and Germany

**1918**
Feb Ration books introduced
Mar German Spring Offensive begins
Nov Armistice

**1919**
Treaty of Versailles

Propaganda succeeded in fuelling anti-German feelings in Britain. In May 1915, the month that the *Lusitania* was sunk, the number of men voluntarily enlisting for the Army increased to 135,000, this was 16,000 more than in April.

Further evidence of anti-German feeling included German Shepherd dogs being officially renamed Alsatians. The British royal family also changed its surname from Saxe-Coburg-Gotha to the more English sounding Windsor in 1917. There were also attacks on German-owned shops and businesses, as Source B shows.

British-produced propaganda toilet paper. It shows an image of the German Kaiser and the quotation 'a scrap of paper', a reference to how Britain's promise to protect Belgium was, mistakenly, viewed in Germany as worthless.

## ACTIVITY

1. a) List the similarities and differences between the presentations of the sinking of the Lusitania in Source A and the medal on page 16.
   b) Try to explain some reasons for any differences.
2. Describe examples of anti-German propaganda featured on these pages.
3. What evidence was there of anti-German feeling in Britain during the War?

▼ **Source B** A crowd of rioters break the windows of a German-owned shop in the East End of London in May 1915 following the sinking of the *Lusitania*.

**1914**
**Aug** War begins
**Aug** Defence of the Realm Act (DORA) passed
**Aug/Sept** Battles of Tannenberg and Masurian Lakes on Eastern Front
**Sept** Trench warfare begins on Western Front

**1915**
**Jan** Poison gas first used
**Apr** Gallipoli campaign begins
**Dec** Siege of Kut begins
Munitions crisis

**1916**
**Jan** Conscription introduced
**Feb** Battle for Verdun begins
**May** Battle of Jutland
**Jul** Battle of the Somme begins

# WHY DID THE SCHLIEFFEN PLAN FAIL?

The German Army invaded Belgium and France in August 1914. French, Belgian and British troops opposed them. At first the German troops made rapid progress, but by the winter, the fighting had developed into static **trench warfare**.

## The Schlieffen Plan: doomed to fail?

Rather than fighting the War from trenches, the German Army had hoped to win a quick victory against France using the Schlieffen Plan (see page 8).

The German Army made good progress to start with. Over 1,500,000 troops advanced through Belgium, forcing French, Belgian and British troops to retreat. But things did not go according to plan, as the map below shows.

▼ The advance and failure of the Schlieffen Plan, August–September 1914.

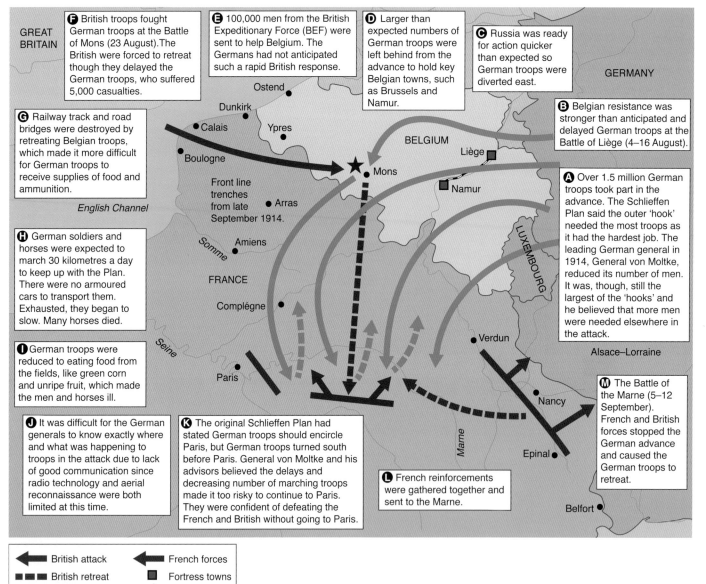

**F** British troops fought German troops at the Battle of Mons (23 August). The British were forced to retreat though they delayed the German troops, who suffered 5,000 casualties.

**E** 100,000 men from the British Expeditionary Force (BEF) were sent to help Belgium. The Germans had not anticipated such a rapid British response.

**D** Larger than expected numbers of German troops were left behind from the advance to hold key Belgian towns, such as Brussels and Namur.

**C** Russia was ready for action quicker than expected so German troops were diverted east.

**B** Belgian resistance was stronger than anticipated and delayed German troops at the Battle of Liège (4–16 August).

**G** Railway track and road bridges were destroyed by retreating Belgian troops, which made it more difficult for German troops to receive supplies of food and ammunition.

**A** Over 1.5 million German troops took part in the advance. The Schlieffen Plan said the outer 'hook' needed the most troops as it had the hardest job. The leading German general in 1914, General von Moltke, reduced its number of men. It was, though, still the largest of the 'hooks' and he believed that more men were needed elsewhere in the attack.

**H** German soldiers and horses were expected to march 30 kilometres a day to keep up with the Plan. There were no armoured cars to transport them. Exhausted, they began to slow. Many horses died.

**I** German troops were reduced to eating food from the fields, like green corn and unripe fruit, which made the men and horses ill.

**J** It was difficult for the German generals to know exactly where and what was happening to troops in the attack due to lack of good communication since radio technology and aerial reconnaissance were both limited at this time.

**K** The original Schlieffen Plan had stated German troops should encircle Paris, but German troops turned south before Paris. General von Moltke and his advisors believed the delays and decreasing number of marching troops made it too risky to continue to Paris. They were confident of defeating the French and British without going to Paris.

**L** French reinforcements were gathered together and sent to the Marne.

**M** The Battle of the Marne (5–12 September). French and British forces stopped the German advance and caused the German troops to retreat.

Legend: British attack — French forces — British retreat — Fortress towns — German attack — Main battles — German retreat

**1917**
Feb British re-take Kut
Apr USA joins the War
Jul Battle of Passchendaele begins
Dec Armistice between Russia and Germany

**1918**
Feb Ration books introduced
Mar German Spring Offensive begins
Nov Armistice

**1919**
Treaty of Versailles

# Digging trenches

As German troops could not continue to advance following the Battle of the Marne (5–12 September 1914), they retreated to more favourable high ground. They began to dig trenches to protect themselves from shrapnel shells, fired from **artillery** such as the French 75 mm field gun (see box below).

Despite their best efforts, the French and British could not dislodge the German troops from their trenches. In turn, British and French troops needed protection from German artillery, so they too dug trenches.

Eventually the trench lines extended from the English Channel to the Swiss border. This became known as the **Western Front**. Neither side moved very far forwards or backwards from these positions until 1918.

## ACTIVITY

1. Make a storyboard of eight drawings with captions to show what happened during the German invasion of Belgium and France.
2. Find examples on pages 18–19 to support each of these reasons why the German invasion failed:
   - The strength of the opposition
   - The problems with supplies
   - The exhaustion and problems of the German troops
   - The decisions made by German generals
   - The limitations of communication
3. Do you think the Schlieffen Plan could ever have worked? Or was it too ambitious and should have anticipated the problems it encountered? Give reasons for your answer.

**Source A** Hermann von Kuhl, a member of the German Army high command during the First World War, writing in 1920. Kuhl was one of General Schlieffen's best pupils. Before the War he was responsible for judging the strength and intentions of Germany's enemies.

I am of the opinion that it would have been possible to have arrived at [victory] in the west in 1914 and that the campaign plan of Schlieffen would have succeeded if only [General von Moltke] had retained it and conducted it as Schlieffen intended.

The French 75 mm field gun, first produced in 1897:
- delivered rapid, accurate fire (6–20 rounds per minute)
- fired shrapnel shells which exploded in the air, releasing hundreds of lead balls causing huge casualties to troops.

In August 1914 the French Army had over 4,000 of these guns.

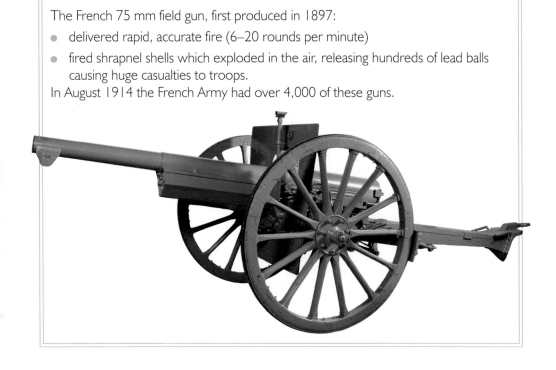

**1914**
**Aug** War begins
**Aug** Defence of the Realm Act (DORA) passed
**Aug/Sept** Battles of Tannenberg and Masurian Lakes on Eastern Front
**Sept** Trench warfare begins on Western Front

**1915**
**Jan** Poison gas first used
**Apr** Gallipoli campaign begins
**Dec** Siege of Kut begins
Munitions crisis

**1916**
**Jan** Conscription introduced
**Feb** Battle for Verdun begins
**May** Battle of Jutland
**Jul** Battle of the Somme begins

# HOW WELL PROTECTED WERE THE TRENCHES?

## Trench systems

Front line trenches directly faced the enemy trenches. Soldiers here had to be constantly on the alert for enemy attacks. Front line trenches were protected by thick rolls of barbed wire and machine guns. Trenches were dug in a zigzag pattern, which minimised the damage caused by shell blasts and prevented bullets being fired down the length of the trench. Sandbags lined trench walls to strengthen them and **dug-outs** provided additional protection. In many German trenches, dug-outs were deep and reinforced with concrete.

Support trenches were positioned behind the front line. But they were close enough that men and supplies could be brought quickly to the front line to help in the event of an attack. Men and supplies were moved through smaller connecting communication trenches that ran parallel to the main trench lines. Behind the support trenches were reserve trenches, and behind these were the heavy artillery – guns with ranges of up to 13 kilometres.

Before an attacking soldier even reached the enemy trenches, he first had to cross **no man's land** – the hostile and barren space between trenches, covered in coils of barbed wire. Where artillery had been active the ground would be cratered with shell holes filled with mud and stagnant water.

A trench system. ▶

Barbed wire: This was a vital part of trench defences.

---

### FRED'S STORY

Captain Fred Sellers was writing to his fiancée Grace Malin in England from the front line in France.

Thursday 21 October 1915
My own dear Gracie
I have just crawled into my dug-out to write a few lines to you … whilst I have been writing shells have been going overhead but not happily dropping on this particular spot – at the moment they have calmed down to one every now and then … This dug-out is fairly roomy [Fred shared it with three other officers] though only high enough to keep one at an uncomfortable bend. It possesses no furniture except a bottle to hold the candle but the sandbags make a comfortable and fairly warm bed … the roof isn't particularly strong but it will stop shrapnel and no roof will stop anything stronger.

**1917**
Feb British re-take Kut
**Apr** USA joins the War
**Jul** Battle of Passchendaele begins
**Dec** Armistice between Russia and Germany

**1918**
**Feb** Ration books introduced
**Mar** German Spring Offensive begins
**Nov** Armistice

**1919**
Treaty of Versailles

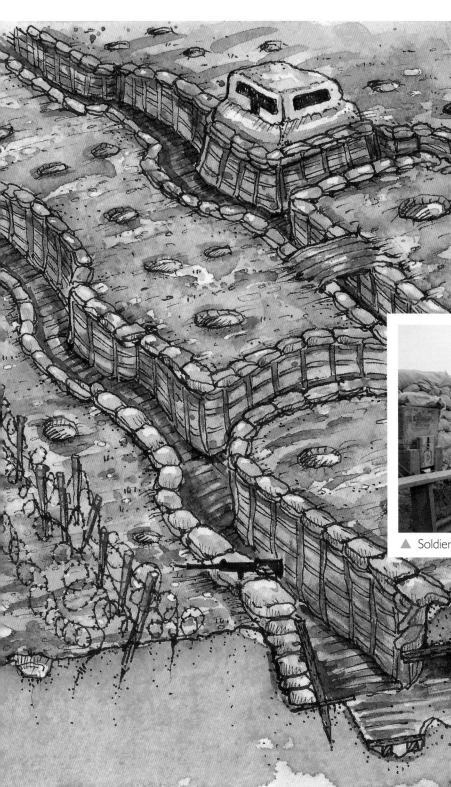

## ACTIVITY

1. On your own copy of the trench diagram, add labels for five of the defensive features explained on these pages.

2. Explain why the following trench features would have caused problems for attacking troops: barbed wire, machine guns, no man's land, zig-zag pattern of trenches, artillery.

3. Think of a method attacking troops might use to overcome each of the main trench defences. You will find out the tactics that were actually used on pages 22–25.

▲ Soldiers in a front line trench.

| 1914 | 1915 | 1916 |
|------|------|------|
| **Aug** War begins | **Jan** Poison gas first used | **Jan** Conscription introduced |
| **Aug** Defence of the Realm Act (DORA) passed | **Apr** Gallipoli campaign begins | **Feb** Battle for Verdun begins |
| **Aug/Sept** Battles of Tannenberg and Masurian Lakes on Eastern Front | **Dec** Siege of Kut begins | **May** Battle of Jutland |
| **Sept** Trench warfare begins on Western Front | Munitions crisis | **Jul** Battle of the Somme begins |

# WHY WAS IT SO DIFFICULT TO ATTACK THE TRENCHES?

An attack usually began with a massive artillery bombardment. This was when long-range artillery fired shells to weaken the enemy trenches and cut their barbed wire defences. Bombardments could last for weeks. The main part of the attack was the infantry advance. Soldiers, sometimes in their thousands, would leave their trenches – going 'over the top', or 'over the bags', to cross no man's land towards the enemy trenches.

From 1916 onwards, friendly artillery frequently fired a **creeping barrage** which was where shells were set to move forward about 90 metres every three minutes, in order to explode just in front of the advancing infantry. The purpose of this was to force the enemy into their dug-outs, making it impossible for them to fire machine guns or rifles at the attacking soldiers.

> **A British Army infantryman went into an attack carrying:**
>
> - wire cutters
> - a gas mask (from 1915 onwards)
> - two hand grenades
> - two empty sandbags
> - 220 rounds of ammunition
> - a Lee-Enfield rifle (typically firing fifteen rounds a minute)
> - a bayonet
> - an entrenching tool (a small portable spade)
> - emergency rations (bully beef and hard biscuits).

## Why did attacks fail?

Artillery bombardments frequently failed to destroy defences, so that advancing infantry had to face uncut barbed wire, machine gun bullets and artillery shells. Artillery was identified as the key to breaking the **stalemate**, but its effective use required huge quantities of ammunition and the production of accurate maps. Creeping barrages often did not properly coordinate with the infantry due to the limitations of communication technology at the time. The result was that sometimes the barrage either advanced too quickly, getting too far ahead of the soldiers, or did not advance quickly enough, shelling their own men. Battles often lasted for weeks and caused thousands of casulties. Successful attacks were difficult to achieve, in large part because of the limited effectiveness of the available weaponry.

> **Source A** Lieutenant J. R. Ackerley, describing taking part in an attack on the first day of the Battle of the Somme on 1 July 1916, in his memoir *My Father and Myself*, published in 1968.
>
> The air when we at last went over the top in broad daylight, positively hummed, buzzed and whined with what sounded like hordes of wasps and hornets but were, of course, bullets … Many of the officers in my battalion were struck down the moment they emerged into view. My company commander was shot through the heart before he had advanced a step.

- Tanks, a new invention, were first used in September 1916 by British forces.
- Armed with guns, machine guns and protected by armour plating, their caterpillar tracks flattened barbed wire and enabled soldiers to cross difficult terrain.
- There were only 49 available the first time they were used in the Battle of the Somme in September 1916 (see pages 24–25) and they frequently broke down.
- The fastest model travelled at 10 kilometres per hour.

▲ Mark V tank, 1918.

**1917**
Feb British re-take Kut
Apr USA joins the War
Jul Battle of Passchendaele begins
Dec Armistice between Russia and Germany

**1918**
Feb Ration books introduced
Mar German Spring Offensive begins
Nov Armistice

**1919**
Treaty of Versailles

During battles, soldiers relied on portable field telephones (used to send speech and **Morse code** messages) which ran on cables that were frequently damaged by shells. New cables had to be laid during an advance; this was a difficult and dangerous task.

Other methods of communication included **runners**, trained dogs, pigeons, **semaphore** and different coloured flares.

## SHELLS

- **Shrapnel shells** contained lead balls that were scattered in mid-air to cause maximum injury to troops. Shrapnel was not particularly effective in destroying trench defences.
- **High explosive shells** exploded when hitting the ground causing substantial damage to trench defences. But these were in short supply at the start of the War (see page 40). The blast was also limited if the shell buried itself before detonating. This was overcome when 'graze fuses' were fitted from 1917, causing shells to explode even on the slightest contact a surface.
- An estimated one in ten shells were duds that failed to explode.

◄ The cross-section and outside of a shrapnel shell.

## GAS

- There were three main types of gas:
  1 Chlorine, first used in April 1915 (caused suffocation).
  2 Phosgene, first used in December 1915 (caused suffocation).
  3 Mustard gas, first used in July 1917 (caused skin burns, blisters and blindness).
- At first, gas was released from canisters and was blown by the wind to reach its target. Shells containing gas which could be fired from artillery were introduced in mid-1916.
- Gas masks were available from April 1915, but were uncomfortable and cumbersome.

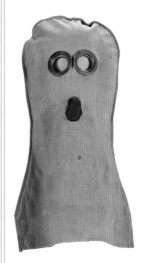

▲ 'Tube' gas mask, adopted in mid-November 1915.

## ACTIVITY

1. Copy and fill in the table below, finding strengths and weaknesses for each strategy.

| Strategy of attack | Strengths of the strategy | Limitations/weaknesses of the strategy |
|---|---|---|
| Artillery bombardment | | |
| Creeping barrage | | |
| Gas attack | | |
| Use of tanks | | |

2. Why do you think the generals failed to come up with many alternative tactics of attack?

**1914**
Aug War begins
Aug Defence of the Realm Act (DORA) passed
Aug/Sept Battles of Tannenberg and Masurian Lakes on Eastern Front
Sept Trench warfare begins on Western Front

**1915**
Jan Poison gas first used
Apr Gallipoli campaign begins
Dec Siege of Kut begins
Munitions crisis

**1916**
Jan Conscription introduced
Feb Battle for Verdun begins
May Battle of Jutland
Jul Battle of the Somme begins

# THE BATTLE OF THE SOMME: A NEEDLESS SLAUGHTER? (1)

On 1 July 1916 British and Empire forces, alongside their French allies, launched a major attack on a 30-kilometre stretch of German trenches near the River Somme in France (see map on page 18).

## Preparations for the attack

A huge preliminary artillery bombardment took place in which 1.5 million shells were fired. This was designed to destroy the German defences and cut through the barbed wire. A week later, at 7.30 a.m. on 1 July, just after a series of large mines had been detonated under the German trench lines, the infantry emerged from their trenches to cross no man's land.

## The first day

It soon became clear that something had gone terribly wrong. German defences were still operating. The artillery bombardment had not worked; it had been spread too thinly. The vulnerable advancing infantry were mowed down in a hail of machine gun fire and shrapnel shells. Most of the British attacks failed. Some men were shot down before they could even cross their own front line trenches. Those who approached the German trenches were stopped by uncut barbed wire in many places. The more experienced French did have successes though, and the British troops nearest them also captured their objectives. The British Army suffered its worst ever losses in a single day. There were almost 60,000 casualties, including 20,000 dead.

## The battle continues

The Battle of the Somme continued without a major breakthrough, then on 15 September the British used a new weapon, the tank, with good results. Although only 49 tanks took part in the attack on the village of Flers, German troops were terrified and retreated. The small number of tanks, however, meant the battle soon slowed to stalemate again. Mud presented another problem. From September, heavy rains combined with the artillery bombardments turned the ground into a bog. It became almost impossible for artillery to be moved, supplies to get through and infantry to advance.

**GEORGE COPPARD'S STORY**

'Hundreds of dead were strung out like wreckage ... Quite as many had died on the enemy wire as on the ground ... they had died on their knees and the wire had prevented their fall ... It was clear that there were no gaps in the wire at the time of the attack ... Had [the British generals] studied the black density of [the wire] through their powerful binoculars? What made them think that artillery fire would pound such wire to pieces? Any Tommy could have told them that shell fire lifts wire up and drops it back down, often in a worse tangle than before.
... What was superior beyond any doubt was the enemy trench system ... [and] any element of surprise ... had been ruined by the long bombardment.'

**GORDON ETHERIDGE'S STORY**

Private Gordon Etheridge, a 24-year-old volunteer soldier from Newfoundland (now part of Canada), took part in the Battle of the Somme. He was part of the Newfoundland Regiment as was his brother, John Charles Etheridge. Their objective was the village of Beaumont Hamel. Gordon Etheridge never reached it.
Of the 780 men in the Newfoundland Regiment, 670 became casualties. Gordon's brother John was seriously injured, and died later of his wounds. Beaumont Hamel was finally captured in the last assault of the Somme in November 1916; by then it was little more than a ruin.

**1917**
Feb British re-take Kut
Apr USA joins the War
Jul Battle of Passchendaele begins
Dec Armistice between Russia and Germany

**1918**
Feb Ration books introduced
Mar German Spring Offensive begins
Nov Armistice

**1919**
Treaty of Versailles

### WILLIAM TICKLE'S STORY

Private William Cecil Tickle from London volunteered, underage, in September 1914. He was only seventeen when he was killed on the third day of the Battle of the Somme, 3 July 1916. This photograph was taken just days before his death. His body was never found; perhaps it was unidentifiable after being hit by a shell or sunk into the mud. His name, along with the names of over 72,000 other 'missing' men, is commemorated on the Thiepval Memorial to the Missing in France.

### WILLIAM'S STORY

William Hamo Vernon volunteered straight from school (see page 13) but died in the Battle of the Somme in 1916, aged 21. His body was never found; his name is commemorated on the Thiepval Memorial to the Missing in France.

## The battle ends

The Battle of the Somme was finally called off in mid-November 1916. German casualties were over 500,000. British and Empire casualties were over 400,000, whilst French losses just exceeded 200,000. The British had gained just 10.5 kilometres at the furthest point of the advance. On page 26 you will find out more to help you decide if there were any winners in this battle.

### ACTIVITY

1. Read George Coppard's Story and the text on page 24. List the difficulties faced by British troops during the Battle of the Somme.

2. Choose the three problems you think were the most significant in causing difficulties for the British troops. Give reasons for your choices.

3. The British generals have sometimes been blamed for the things that went wrong during the Battle of the Somme. Write down why you think they might have been blamed. You will find out whether such criticisms were fair on pages 26–27.

▼ **Source A** Horses knee-deep in mud, struggling to transport ammunition at the Somme, outside Flers, November 1916.

| 1914 | 1915 | 1916 |
|---|---|---|
| **Aug** War begins<br>**Aug** Defence of the Realm Act (DORA) passed<br>**Aug/Sept** Battles of Tannenberg and Masurian Lakes on Eastern Front<br>**Sept** Trench warfare begins on Western Front | **Jan** Poison gas first used<br>**Apr** Gallipoli campaign begins<br>**Dec** Siege of Kut begins<br>Munitions crisis | **Jan** Conscription introduced<br>**Feb** Battle for Verdun begins<br>**May** Battle of Jutland<br>**Jul** Battle of the Somme begins |

# THE BATTLE OF THE SOMME: A NEEDLESS SLAUGHTER? (2)

The Battle of the Somme caused the most casualties of any single battle during the entire War – with casualties from all sides totalling 1.2 million. Some historians have blamed the Commander-in-Chief of the British Army, Douglas Haig, for this; condemning him as old-fashioned and indifferent to the sufferings of the troops.

Haig has been criticised for:

The preliminary artillery bombardment, which failed to destroy the German defences.

Repeatedly sending large numbers of infantry in advances across no man's land, even when this didn't seem to be working.

▲ Douglas Haig, 1917.

The failure to make enough use of new technology, especially tanks.

Not calling off the battle until November, despite the huge losses.

## Why did Haig act as he did at the Somme?

Are the criticisms of Haig fair? Or were his tactical options limited by available resources and technology, and by events outside of his control? Here are some facts about Haig and the Battle of the Somme to help you decide:

**FACT 1:**
British intelligence reports during the battle said the German Army was about to collapse.

**FACT 2:**
Allied attacks continued until November, long after it was clear that the Allies were not advancing.

**FACT 3:**
A significant proportion of shells were duds (see page 23).

**FACT 4:**
Tanks were used for the first time in battle. Haig had been promised 150 tanks by June 1916. By September 1916 only 49 were available, and they tended to be unreliable and slow (see page 22).

**FACT 5:**
Low cloud in the days before the attack began made it impossible for British **reconnaissance aircraft** to see if the barbed wire and German defences had been destroyed.

**FACT 6:**
In February 1916, German troops attacked the French Army at Verdun (see map on page 18). French casualties were enormous and if France was defeated here it would have weakened the entire Western Front. A British attack would force the Germans to divert many of their troops away from Verdun.

**FACT 7:**
Haig's subordinate officers, who were responsible for the battle on the ground, did not always manage the fighting exactly as Haig would have wanted.

**FACT 8:**
It was difficult to communicate with soldiers during an attack because of the technology.

**FACT 9:**
The German trenches were deep, and often reinforced with concrete.

**FACT 10:**
Less effective shrapnel shells were often used in artillery bombardments since than high explosive shells were in short supply.

**1917**
Feb British re-take Kut
Apr USA joins the War
Jul Battle of Passchendaele begins
Dec Armistice between Russia and Germany

**1918**
Feb Ration books introduced
Mar German Spring Offensive begins
Nov Armistice

**1919**
Treaty of Versailles

# Who 'won' the Battle of the Somme?

The Somme did not bring the decisive result the Allies had hoped for. But the battle did change things. The Germans were forced to move troops to the Somme, limiting the resources they had available to continue their assault on Verdun. German soldiers who fought on the Somme were horrified and demoralised by the intensity of the attack. This was the first time which they had experienced Allied firepower on this scale. The cost had been terrible and the suffering of all sides had been immense. It had become clear that there could be no victory without further loss of lives on a huge scale. However, only a minority of people at the time publicly questioned whether it was worth paying such a price.

**Source B** Haig writing in his diary following a meeting with the leader of the French Army, Joseph Joffre, on 26 May 1916, at which they discussed possible dates for a British attack on the Somme.

The moment I mentioned 15 August, Joffre at once got very excited and shouted that 'The French Amy would cease to exist, if we did nothing till then!' … I pointed out that in spite of … 15 August being the most favourable for the British army to take action, … in view of what he … said regarding the unfortunate condition of the French army, I was prepared to commence operations on 1 July.

**Source A** Haig's public message summarising his view of the War, published in the *London Gazette* newspaper, 10 April 1919.

Immense as the influence of mechanical devices might be, they cannot by themselves decide a campaign. Their true role is that of assisting the infantryman, which they have done in a most admirable manner. They cannot replace him. Only by the rifle and bayonet of the infantryman can the decisive victory be won.

## ACTIVITY

1. a) Find evidence from pages 26–27 to support these general criticisms of Haig as:
   - old-fashioned and unimaginative
   - indifferent to the sufferings of his men.
   b) How might Haig defend himself from these criticisms?
2. What is your view of Haig as a commander? Prepare a speech that either condemns or defends Haig for his tactics during the Battle of the Somme. Give evidence to support your arguments.
3. 'The Battle of the Somme was a pointless waste of lives and should never have been fought.' Do you agree with this statement? Why/why not?

▼ **Source C** A broken-down Mark I tank, on its way to attack Thiepval during the Battle of the Somme, September 1916.

# ALLIED ATTACKS ON THE OTTOMAN EMPIRE: REALISTIC OR OPTIMISTIC?

Fighting did not just take place on the Western Front. The huge **Ottoman Empire** entered the War on Germany's side in November 1914. In 1915, British and Empire forces launched two attacks: one at Gallipoli, the other in **Mesopotamia** (now Iraq, see maps on p.57). Both were ambitious, but what were the chances of success? Judge for yourself as you find out about the terrain, Turkish defences, and the strength of British and Empire forces.

## The Gallipoli Campaign

The British plan was to gain control of the Dardanelles Straits. It was hoped this would contribute to forcing the Ottoman Empire to surrender. Control of the Dardanelles would also open up a vital sea supply route through which supplies could be sent to the struggling Russian Army.

Sea mines prevented the battleships from sailing through the Straits and smaller mine sweeping vessels could not remove the mines as they were bombarded by guns fired from Turkish forts on the cliffs of the Gallipoli peninsula. Infantry landings on Gallipoli would be needed to take control of these forts and silence the guns. How likely were these landings to succeed given the situation in 1915?

### THE TURKISH ARMY

The Turkish Army in 1915:

- had 150,000 troops in peace time, increasing to 800,000 when at war
- had ineffective conscription; at least 25 per cent of recruits refused to serve each year
- had been recently defeated in the Balkan Wars (1912–13) by Serbia, Bulgaria, Greece and Montenegro
- lacked modern weapons at the start of the War, although Germany did send some supplies from 1914
- had recently undergone military reforms to modernise the army
- had to fight the Allies in four different parts of its Empire by 1915.

### The situation 1915

The British had 75,000 troops and 77 ships available for the invasion; most of these were inexperienced in combat.

Allied minesweepers had not removed the sea mines.

A naval bombardment in February 1915 failed to destroy the Turkish forts.

It was likely that Turkish forces would have reinforced their defences following the naval attack.

The British did not have detailed maps of the peninsula's terrain.

British intelligence in December 1914 estimated 27,000 of the Turkish forces were at Gallipoli, but the true number was unknown.

Ships could use large guns to fire on Turkish forts (although not necessarily accurately).

No portable wireless radios existed for communication between troops.

All supplies (weapons, ammunition, food and water) would have to be shipped in and landed on the beaches.

The terrain off the beaches was steep and rocky.

The water near the beach was very shallow; troops would have to land from rowing boats.

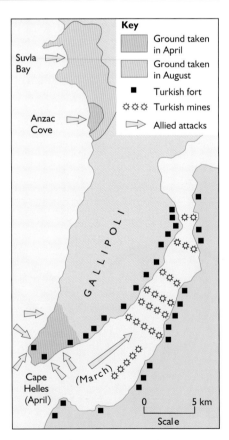

**Key**
- Ground taken in April
- Ground taken in August
- ■ Turkish fort
- ✿✿✿ Turkish mines
- ⇨ Allied attacks

Suvla Bay

Anzac Cove

GALLIPOLI

Cape Helles (April)

(March)

0    5 km

Scale

▲ Turkish defences around Gallipoli.

**1917**
Feb British re-take Kut
Apr USA joins the War
Jul Battle of Passchendaele begins
Dec Armistice between Russia and Germany

**1918**
Feb Ration books introduced
Mar German Spring Offensive begins
Nov Armistice

**1919**
Treaty of Versailles

# The Baghdad Campaign

In Mesopotamia, British and British Empire forces were based in Kuwait, a British **protectorate** and a source of important oil supplies. The British gradually extended their control in the area and decided to send a force to capture Baghdad in November 1915. General Sir John Nixon, the commander in Mesopotamia, was confident of success. Was this optimism fair or foolish, given that the following was the situation in 1915?

## The situation in 1915

The British, had successfully occupied Basra (450 kilometres from Baghdad) in November 1914 with minimal resistance and the fortified town of Kut-al-Amara (64 kilometres south of Baghdad) in September 1915.

Most essential supplies needed to be transported from Basra.

British intelligence estimates of the numbers of Turkish troops in the region varied hugely from 9,000 to 50,000.

General Nixon had been promised 20,000 extra men from the Western Front to take part in the attack. They never arrived.

Supply routes frequently came under attack.

Diseases like dysentery, cholera, typhoid and malaria were common in Mesopotamia.

The River Tigris was vital for the transporting supplies. In November 1915, the water level was so low that the British could only use flat-bottomed boats. They only had fourteen such boats.

The main British Empire force available in the region was the 6th Indian Division – 11,000 troops led by Major General Townshend. He thought an attack on Baghdad was unlikely to succeed.

In summertime, temperatures could rise to over 45 degrees for ten hours a day.

---

**ACTIVITY**

1. Read the box on page 28 about the Turkish Army. Why might the British have believed the Turkish Army would be easy to defeat in early 1915?
2. a) Copy and complete the table below.

|  | Likely to succeed | Difficult but not necessarily unlikely to succeed | Unlikely to succeed |
|---|---|---|---|
| Gallipoli Campaign |  |  |  |
| Baghdad Campaign |  |  |  |

   b) Try to group the reasons in the table above into categories. E.g. *reasons to do with poor planning*.
3. On the continuum below, mark 'Gallipoli Campaign' and 'Baghdad Campaign' to show how far you believe the British were realistically hopeful or foolishly optimistic. Give reasons for your view.

**Realistically hopeful**                                    **Foolishly optimistic**

| 1914 | 1915 | 1916 |
|---|---|---|
| **Aug** War begins | **Jan** Poison gas first used | **Jan** Conscription introduced |
| **Aug** Defence of the Realm Act (DORA) passed | **Apr** Gallipoli campaign begins | **Feb** Battle for Verdun begins |
| **Aug/Sept** Battles of Tannenberg and Masurian Lakes on Eastern Front | **Dec** Siege of Kut begins | **May** Battle of Jutland |
| **Sept** Trench warfare begins on Western Front | Munitions crisis | **Jul** Battle of the Somme begins |

# WHAT WENT WRONG WITH THE ALLIED ATTACKS?

## The Gallipoli Campaign

The infantry attack began on 25 April 1915. Troops were landed on a number of Gallipoli beaches. The objective was to destroy Turkish defences and eventually take over the entire peninsula.

Turkish resistance was stronger than expected. Many troops were met by machine gunfire as they struggled to get ashore. The steep climb up the cliffs from many of the landing beaches caused further difficulties with soldiers becoming exhausted, lost or split up. Turkish troops, hidden in the thick thorny bushes, fired at the troops and added to the confusion.

ANZAC (Australian and New Zealand Army Corps) officers knew that taking the high ground of the ridge was important but they did not get a chance to do this before Turkish reinforcements arrived by the afternoon. This also prevented ANZACs joining up with British troops further south.

After they failed to destroy Turkish defences, Allied troops had little choice but to dig shallow trenches to provide some shelter from Turkish gunfire. As on the Western Front, unintended trench warfare began. Substantial reinforcements were sent, but the Allies were unable to break out of their trenches.

In the summer heat, decomposing corpses, overflowing latrines and flies contributed to the spread of disease, in particular dysentery. Twenty-two per cent of British and Empire forces became so ill that they had to be evacuated.

In December 1915 all troops were finally evacuated. Almost one in three British and Empire troops at Gallipoli had been killed or wounded.

**Source A** Lieutenant Colonel Mustafa Kemal, a Turkish general at Gallipoli, recounts in his memoirs the order he gave to his commanders on 25 April 1915 when he refused to let them retreat from the invading ANZACs.

I don't order you to attack – I order you to die. In the time which passes until we die, other troops and commanders can take our places.

**Source B** Brigadier General Sir Hugh Simpson-Baikie, British artillery commander at Gallipoli in 1915.

The complete absence of High Explosive [shells] was severely felt, as shrapnel [shells] were of little use for destroying trenches … We had no heavy guns capable of replying to the Turkish heavy guns … from whose fire our infantry suffered severely. My feelings as an artillery commander, unable to give them anything like the support they would have had in France or **Flanders**, may be guessed.

### REGINALD'S STORY

A volunteer from Australia, Reginald Roy Inwood, was one of the large number of Australian and New Zealand Army Corps (ANZAC) troops who took part in the attack on Gallipoli. He had enlisted at the age of 24. At the time he had been working as a miner near Adelaide. Roy fought in Gallipoli until November 1915 during which time he was promoted from Private to Lance Corporal. He was then sent to the Western Front in France, where he was awarded the Victoria Cross in 1917 for bravery. His brother, Robert, was killed in action in France.

### IVOR'S STORY

Ivor Evans was just fifteen when he enlisted in 1914 (see page 12). He served in Gallipoli, Greece and France. While overseas he suffered badly from dysentery and frostbite and was sent back to Britain to recover. He returned to fight in France, but was killed on 23 November 1917, aged only eighteen. He is buried in Hargicourt British Military Cemetery in France.

1917
**Feb** British re-take Kut
**Apr** USA joins the War
**Jul** Battle of Passchendaele begins
**Dec** Armistice between Russia and Germany

1918
**Feb** Ration books introduced
**Mar** German Spring Offensive begins
**Nov** Armistice

1919
Treaty of Versailles

# The Baghdad Campaign

British and Empire troops were outnumbered by Turkish forces and halted on their march to Baghdad at the Battle of Ctesiphon in November 1915. The British suffered 4,600 casualties. Major General Townshend knew they were critically short of medical and food supplies due to problems with the supply routes (see page 29), and decided to retreat to Kut-al-Amara. The Turkish forces pursued them and, in December 1915, began a siege of the town.

British and Empire forces suffered terribly from hunger and disease, slaughtering their own horses for food. Large British forces were sent but failed to break the siege. After five months, in April 1916, Major General Townshend surrendered unconditionally. All troops from the British and Empire forces became prisoners; over 4,000 of them would die in captivity.

In February 1917, a well supplied British Empire force of 150,000 recaptured Kut-al-Amara. They went on to take Baghdad in March 1917.

**Source C** Edward Mousley, a captain in the Royal Field Artillery, was besieged at Kut-al-Amara. He describes the conditions in the town in March 1916 in his memoirs which were written during his time as a prisoner of the Ottoman Empire between 1916 and 1918.

Rations have been still further cut down … We get bread and meat, nothing else, and of the former merely four ounces [about 2 slices] per day. The garrison is in a bad way. Men go staggering about … We are a sick army, a skeleton army rocking with cholera and disease.

## ACTIVITY

1. a) Create a storyboard of six pictures with captions to show what happened during the Gallipoli Campaign.
   b) Create a storyboard of six pictures with captions to show what happened during the Baghdad Campaign.
2. Use the information from pages 28–31 to provide evidence to complete the table below. You may not find evidence for every box.

|  | Gallipoli Campaign | Baghdad Campaign |
|---|---|---|
| Poor planning and leadership |  |  |
| Strong enemy resistance |  |  |
| Difficult terrain and climate |  |  |
| Disease |  |  |

3. Sources A, B and C were written by people who took part in the campaigns. Does this make them reliable as evidence about why the campaigns failed?

**Source D** A stretcher being carried ▶ through a trench at Gallipoli.

**1914**
Aug War begins
Aug Defence of the Realm Act (DORA) passed
Aug/Sept Battles of Tannenberg and Masurian Lakes on Eastern Front
Sept Trench warfare begins on Western Front

**1915**
Jan Poison gas first used
Apr Gallipoli campaign begins
Dec Siege of Kut begins
   Munitions crisis

**1916**
Jan Conscription introduced
Feb Battle for Verdun begins
May Battle of Jutland
Jul Battle of the Somme begins

# WHAT WERE CONDITIONS LIKE IN THE TRENCHES ON THE WESTERN FRONT?

On the Western Front, both sides built enormous networks of trenches. Front line trenches were those directly facing the enemy. Behind these were support and reserve trenches (see page 20).

## Sandbags

Sandbags were a vital part of the trenches. They stopped the sides from collapsing and provided protection from bullets and shell blasts. The British used around 1.3 billion sandbags during the War.

## Duckboards

Trench floors could fill quickly with water and mud in rainy conditions. This was especially true in Belgium, where the soil was mainly clay and did not easily absorb water. Men used duckboards (wooden planks nailed together) to help their feet stay dry and prevent trench foot. This was a fungal infection brought on by the constant immersion of feet in the water of flooded trenches. In severe cases men had to have their feet amputated. As the War progressed, trench foot became less of a problem as a result of increased use of duckboards and regular foot inspections when men could change their footwear and sometimes apply whale oil to protect their feet.

1  Wrapping food
2  Protecting rifles from mud and dust
3  Camouflaging shiny steel helmets (from 1916 onwards)
4  Tablecloth
5  Towel
6  Wrapping round trousers to stop them getting caked in mud
7  Emergency bandage
8  Sewn together as a shroud for the dead
9  Cloak against the rain
10 Cover to protect bayonets from rust

▲ Ten uses for a sandbag.

▼ **Source A** Officers of the 12th Royal Irish Rifles wading through mud in a trench. Essigny, France.

1917
Feb British re-take Kut
Apr USA joins the War
Jul Battle of Passchendaele begins
Dec Armistice between Russia and Germany

1918
Feb Ration books introduced
Mar German Spring Offensive begins
Nov Armistice

1919
Treaty of Versailles

**Source B** Sergeant Harry Roberts, a soldier with the Lancashire Fusiliers, in an interview after the War.

If you have never had trench feet described to you. I will tell you. Your feet swell to two or three times their normal size and go completely dead. You could stick a bayonet into them and not feel a thing. If you are fortunate enough not to lose your feet and the swelling begins to go down, it is then that the intolerable, indescribable agony begins. I have heard men cry and even scream with the pain and many had to have their feet and legs amputated.

**Source C** The nineteen-year-old officer Graham Greenwell wrote about being shelled in the trenches in a letter to his mother during the War.

It is sitting still throughout a solid day listening to the shells wondering if the next will be on the dug-out or not which is so unnerving ... of course, at the end the ones who are alive are absolutely demoralised.

# Dug-outs

Initially, dug-outs were just small holes dug out of the sides of trench walls to provide a bit of shelter from shell blasts and a place to rest. As the War progressed, they became larger and so gave more protection. Officers' dug-outs were often tunnelled down into the ground, walled with sandbags and roofed with timber and earth. Dug-outs provided some protection against shrapnel, but not against a direct hit by a shell.

# Trench pests

Various animals and insects lived in the trenches along with the soldiers. These included large brown rats, flies, mosquitoes and lice. The lice got into the clothes of the men and their bites caused terrible itching.

# Snipers

There was a significant risk of being shot by an enemy **sniper** while in a front line trench. One British officer estimated that, in 1915, German snipers were killing eighteen British soldiers a day. Soldiers tried to find the position of persistent enemy snipers by using dummy heads which they raised above the trenches so that the dummies were shot. When these were hit, the soldiers could use the angle of the bullet to guess the sniper's position.

## GEORGE COPPARD'S STORY

'A full day's rest allowed us to clean up a bit and to launch a full scale attack on lice. I sat in a quiet corner for about two hours delousing myself as best I could. We were all at it, for none of us escaped their vile attentions. The blighters [got into] the seams of trousers ... and seemed impregnable. In parcels from home it was usual to receive a tin of supposed death-dealing powder but the lice [seemed to] thrive on the stuff.'

## ACTIVITY

1. Describe the main purpose of the following trench features: sandbags, duckboards, dug-outs.
2. Describe five of the main difficulties and dangers of trench life explained on these pages.
3. Create a survival guide for use by troops in the trenches. You should include descriptions of the main dangers and difficulties, and instructions about what methods can be used to minimise these dangers (see pages 20–23 and this spread, pages 32–33.)

◀ **Source D** A trench sign warning of snipers.

1914
Aug War begins
Aug Defence of the Realm Act (DORA) passed
Aug/Sept Battles of Tannenberg and Masurian Lakes on Eastern Front
Sept Trench warfare begins on Western Front

1915
Jan Poison gas first used
Apr Gallipoli campaign begins
Dec Siege of Kut begins
Munitions crisis

1916
Jan Conscription introduced
Feb Battle for Verdun begins
May Battle of Jutland
Jul Battle of the Somme begins

# TRENCH LIFE ON THE WESTERN FRONT: '90 PER CENT ROUTINE, 10 PER CENT TERROR'?

There was a strict routine to life in the trenches on the Western Front. On the right is a typical timetable for a soldier in the trenches.

## Work

To maintain strong, secure trenches, soldiers needed to carry out these essential jobs:

- repairing trench walls
- filling sandbags
- draining trenches
- digging trenches
- laying barbed wire
- transporting food and ammunition into the trenches.

These last three were particularly dangerous due to the risks from enemy snipers and shells, and were usually safest done at night.

## Food

Front line soldiers were recommended a daily intake of 4,193 calories because of the physical work they carried out. They were also meant to eat one hot meal a day. However due to difficulties in transporting this from behind the lines where it was prepared, soldiers at the Front relied primarily on tinned rations. There was a good supply of bully beef and jam (almost always plum and apple) as well as hard, dry biscuits. Fresh rations of meat, cheese, bread and vegetables were supplied when possible. Water was usually transported in empty petrol tins (it never completely lost this unpleasant taste). It was then sterilised for drinking.

Food parcels sent by families to their loved ones in the trenches were always popular.

| TIME | ACTIVITY |
|---|---|
| 5am | 'Stand-to'/'stand to arms' – soldiers lined up, fully armed, for inspection every morning one hour before dawn (the most likely time for an enemy attack). |
| 8am | Breakfast |
| 9am | Fatigues – these were jobs that needed doing to maintain trenches (see section on 'Work'). |
| 12 noon | Lunch |
| 1pm | Sentry duty – sentries observed no man's land and enemy trenches using trench periscopes |
| 3pm | Rest |
| 6pm | Dinner |
| 7pm | 'Stand-to' |
| 8pm | Fatigues |
| 10pm | Sentry duty |
| 12 midnight | Rest |
| 2am | Sentry duty |
| 4am | Rest |

A typical timetable for ▶ a front line soldier.

A tin of Maconochie, a beef and vegetable mix. This and 'bully beef' (corned beef) were the most common tinned food.

An army biscuit, with a witty inscription. It reads 'King and country need you and this is how they feed you'.

**1917**
Feb British re-take Kut
Apr USA joins the War
Jul Battle of Passchendaele begins
Dec Armistice between Russia and Germany

**1918**
Feb Ration books introduced
Mar German Spring Offensive begins
Nov Armistice

**1919**
Treaty of Versailles

# Rest

Typically, soldiers were allowed two hours of rest for every four hours of work. When the soldiers were not actually trying to sleep, many read magazines, played cards, or wrote letters home. These letters were **censored** to remove any important military information. Some soldiers invented secret codes to let their relatives know where they were, such as putting small dots under certain letters to spell out a location.

Soldiers would usually spend four to nine days in the trenches per month, and just two or three of these in a front line trench. This rotation was vital for maintaining **morale**. The rest of the time, soldiers were stationed behind the trench lines in nearby towns and villages, often sleeping in barns or tents. Although they still had to exercise and carry out fatigues, they could also spend time in the towns, for instance, going to the cinema.

Home leave, however, was rare: officers tended to get it every seven months, soldiers every fourteen months. It was particularly precious to Captain Fred Sellers who married Grace Malin on 15 December 1917, during his leave.

## ACTIVITY

1. Write a soldier's timetable. This should be based on the example on page 34 but include specific examples of work done and food eaten at each meal.

2. Read Fred's Story on this page. Complete the table below to show what Fred says about trench life and how much other evidence there is to support his view. An example is shown in the table.

| What Fred says about trench life | Other evidence that backs up what Fred says |
|---|---|
| Ate hard biscuits in the trenches | Hard army biscuits were everyday rations in the trenches |
| | |

3. A common view of life in the trenches is that 'soldiers spent long amounts of time in the trenches, were in constant danger of being shot, and had to survive on very little, tasteless food'. Is this an accurate view? Give reasons for your answer.

## FRED'S STORY

**Thursday 28 October 1915**
Dear Grace
… The chocolate arrived today, you know Gracie how I appreciate the fact that you would send me anything I wanted. Your last chocolate really became an emergency ration for me. After having no food all day and no prospect of any all night – I ate some of it with those [hard] biscuits – almost dog biscuits – which I found. That was in the trenches … [But] As a rule we are remarkably well fed … I know that you would be perfectly ashamed of me for even in a month I have become enormously fatter. I am sincerely hoping I have become considerably more normal before I see you again … Always, Fred.
P.S. I hope you are knitting more socks – please Gracie.

**14 June 1916**
The other evening [when stationed behind the lines] I strolled into the neighbouring town by myself and [went] to a cinema for an hour. I saw [a] Charles Chaplin [film] … and a few wild westerns. Cinemas are great things to have behind the line … it is surprising how far a cinema film can take one, and two hours later be in the trenches … goodbye darling, Fred.

1914
Aug War begins
Aug Defence of the Realm Act (DORA) passed
Aug/Sept Battles of Tannenberg and Masurian Lakes on Eastern Front
Sept Trench warfare begins on Western Front

1915
Jan Poison gas first used
Apr Gallipoli campaign begins
Dec Siege of Kut begins
Munitions crisis

1916
Jan Conscription introduced
Feb Battle for Verdun begins
May Battle of Jutland
Jul Battle of the Somme begins

# HOW DID LIFE ON DIFFERENT FRONTS COMPARE?

Soldiers experienced the War very differently depending on where in the world they were sent. The majority of British troops fought in France and Belgium (the Western Front), but they also served alongside British Empire troops in Mesopotamia, Egypt, Palestine, Gallipoli, Italy and Africa. A soldier's chance of survival differed considerably from region to region; approximately 11 per cent of soldiers sent to France and Flanders died, 10 per cent of those who were sent to Mesopotamia and 5.6 per cent of those at Gallipoli never returned.

Key factors affecting this were climate and disease. During the War, more deaths were caused by disease than by enemy action. Climate had an enormous impact on soldiers' lives as they often had to live outdoors. Soldiers in all regions suffered from ill health and disease, but some problems were specific to particular regions and climates as the graph and clipboard on the right and below show.

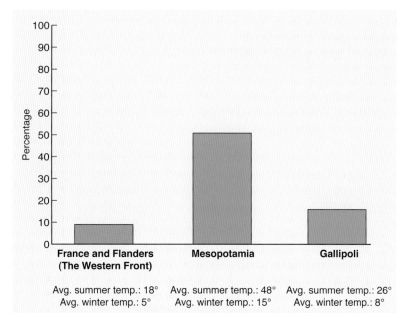

| | France and Flanders (The Western Front) | Mesopotamia | Gallipoli |
|---|---|---|---|
| Avg. summer temp. | 18° | 48° | 26° |
| Avg. winter temp. | 5° | 15° | 8° |

▲ The average temperatures and percentage of total deaths of British or Empire soldiers who died from causes other than enemy action for each region.

▼ **Source A** British troops in Mesopotamia hauling a gun, wearing sun helmets and pads of cloth over their spines which they believed protected them against sunstroke.

**Information about diseases**

• Sandfly fever: caused by bites from infected sandflies, causing high temperatures and muscle aches. Mainly affected troops in Mesopotamia.
• Heatstroke: caused by extreme hot weather, causing the body to overheat. Can be fatal. Affected troops in Mesopotamia (see Source A).
• Bronchitis and pneumonia: diseases often made worse by damp and cold conditions, caused breathing difficulties. Mainly affected troops on the Western Front.
• Frostbite: caused by exposure to extreme cold, damaged the skin and sometimes muscle tissue, usually of the hands and feet. Mainly affected troops on the Western Front (see Source C), though troops in Gallipoli also suffered.
• Trench foot (see page 32): mostly affected troops on the Western Front.
• Lice: caused significant itching and the bites could become infected. Lived in clothes and on skin. Affected troops in all regions.
• Dysentery: caused by consuming contaminated food and water. Affected troops in all regions but a particular problem in Gallipoli, where huge numbers of flies during the summer spread the infection (see Source D).

**1917**
Feb British re-take Kut
Apr USA joins the War
Jul Battle of Passchendaele begins
Dec Armistice between Russia and Germany

**1918**
Feb Ration books introduced
Mar German Spring Offensive begins
Nov Armistice

**1919**
Treaty of Versailles

# Fresh foods

Standard tinned rations (see page 34), although repetitive and bland, provided enough calories for soldiers. When available, local fresh food supplemented the tins. The fresh food varied from region to region. For instance, you could find:

- melons, cucumbers and dates in Mesopotamia
- apples, carrots and fresh eggs in Belgium and France.

In Gallipoli, troops often struggled to get fresh food to their hillside trenches on the peninsula. They received additional Marmite in their rations due to its high levels of vitamin B.

For the troops trapped for five months in Kut-al-Amara (see page 31), all food was in dangerously short supply. Soldiers were forced to slaughter their own horses for meat.

**ACTIVITY**

1.  Using the Sources and information on these pages, compare the key features of life on different Fronts by completing this table:

| | Climate | Health conditions and diseases | Food |
|---|---|---|---|
| Mesopotamia | | | |
| Gallipoli | | | |
| Belgium and France | | | |

2.  Read Sources A, B, C and D. Identify and describe the main difficulties or complaints being made in each Source.
3.  Where would you have *least* wanted to have been sent?
    - Mesopotamia
    - Gallipoli
    - Belgium/France

    Explain your answer in a paragraph which includes information about: death rates, climate, food, and ill health/ disease. You could also include information about the type of fighting in the region.

**Source C** Ganga Dut, an Indian officer in the British and Empire forces, writing from France to his family in the Punjab on 31 January 1917.

At the present time the cold is more intense than can be described. If you pour hot water on the ground it immediately becomes like *ghi* [a hard butter used in Indian cooking]. This is my third winter in this country; but it has never before been as cold as it is now … Still, all the men are well and happy. We get good rations, and sufficient … Although the cold is so severe, there is no sickness, except discomfort of the feet. Many men get their feet swollen through the cold.

**Source D** Gunner Dudley Meneaud-Lissenburg, serving with the Royal Field Artillery in Gallipoli, remembered the swarms of flies there in May 1915.

We were invaded by millions of flies … Drinking and eating was a real nightmare and I avoided, no matter how hungry I was, rice pudding [which was] mixed with currants. It was difficult to distinguish currants from flies. The flies would swarm down and many of them would fall into the pudding. The spreading of jam onto a hardtack biscuit was indeed a frustrating exercise; [three men were needed] one to open the tin, another to flick away the flies and a third to spread the jam and cover the biscuit.

**Source B** Soldiers in a snowy trench in France 1917. The winter of 1917 was exceptionally cold, with an evening temperature of −14°C recorded in Paris.

**1914**
**Aug** War begins
**Aug** Defence of the Realm Act (DORA) passed
**Aug/Sept** Battles of Tannenberg and Masurian Lakes on Eastern Front
**Sept** Trench warfare begins on Western Front

**1915**
**Jan** Poison gas first used
**Apr** Gallipoli campaign begins
**Dec** Siege of Kut begins
Munitions crisis

**1916**
**Jan** Conscription introduced
**Feb** Battle for Verdun begins
**May** Battle of Jutland
**Jul** Battle of the Somme begins

# HOW DID PEOPLE 'DO THEIR BIT' FOR THE WAR?

The War placed huge demands on everyone, including those at home in Britain. People were affected by shortages, by the absence of the men now fighting at the Front, and by the demands of producing war materials on an enormous scale.

The British government passed the Defence of the Realm Act (DORA) in 1914 which gave them powers to control many aspects of people's daily lives in order to protect Britain and the war effort. Unprecedented government control was also imposed on the industry and the workforce (see pages 40–41).

But the government also appealed for people to voluntarily 'do their bit' to help. Many people responded by giving donations, sending parcels or working to support the War effort.

## Charities

People could help to support wartime charities through voluntary work or donations. These charities supported a wide range of causes including: serving soldiers, injured soldiers, war widows, orphans, refugees and injured military animals. Over 18,000 new charities and special funds were set up during the War on top of those already established, like the Red Cross.

▲ **Source B** A poster appealing for donations of fresh eggs which were not often available for soldiers at the Front. The fund, established in August 1915, was very successful, often collecting over a million eggs a month for serving or wounded soldiers.

**Source A** John Reith, a young officer in the War, describes receiving an unexpected parcel in the trenches, in his memoir *Wearing Spurs*, published in 1966.

One evening a splendid box of candy arrived from a girl of whom I had never heard: others followed from her at regular intervals … [the explanation was that] shortly after we had gone overseas a photograph of the officers was published in a Glasgow newspaper. This young lady and some friends allocated us out among themselves with this highly satisfactory result. I never met her.

**Source C** Captain John Liddell, writing to his family in November 1914, criticising the contents of some of the charitable parcels sent to soldiers.

The people who send them [parcels of hand-knitted clothes] mean very well, but … some of the efforts that arrive are very thin and shoddy. Especially do I condemn the atrocity known as the heelless sock.

Souvenir cufflinks made from pieces of a German **zeppelin** shot down over England in 1916. They were sold to raise money for the Red Cross which provided medical aid to troops. Zeppelin raids over England accounted for the deaths of 1,413 deaths in Britain during the War. People were deeply shocked to become targets in their own homes.

**1917**
Feb British re-take Kut
Apr USA joins the War
Jul Battle of Passchendaele begins
Dec Armistice between Russia and Germany

**1918**
Feb Ration books introduced
Mar German Spring Offensive begins
Nov Armistice

**1919**
Treaty of Versailles

# War bonds

People could help fund the war effort, and make a small profit, by purchasing **war bonds**. In return for their money, the buyer received a paper guarantee from the government promising to repay the cost of the bond plus interest after the War. It was a secure and patriotic way for people to invest, and increased the funds for the government to spend on weapons during the War.

# Working women

Women were a huge potential source of labour, but strict attitudes about what was appropriate work limited the jobs women were permitted to do. A woman's proper place was regarded as being in the home, as a wife and mother. Nevertheless, many women did work, mainly single and working class women. But they tended to be employed in traditional female roles such as maids and nurses or in teaching or textiles.

**FLORENCE'S STORY**

Florence Farmborough was 27 and living in Moscow and working as an English tutor to a wealthy Russian family when the War broke out. She volunteered for service, training as a Red Cross nurse. She was sent to the Eastern Front (in Russia and what is now the Ukraine and Poland) where Russian forces were fighting against German troops.

▼ **Source E** A tram driver and conductor in Scotland during the War.

▲ **Source D** Workers sealing tins of army biscuits at a factory in Lancashire.

**ACTIVITY**

1. a) How might people in Britain have helped each of the following:
   - A soldier at the front line?
   - A wounded soldier in hospital?
   b) Design a poster for a wartime charity appealing for donations.
2. a) List the ways in which women helped to support the war effort.
   b) Which of the roles in your list were a challenge to the traditional views of acceptable women's work?
   c) How important do you think the War was in changing people's attitudes towards women's work?

| 1914 | | 1915 | | 1916 | |
|---|---|---|---|---|---|

**1914**
**Aug** War begins
**Aug** Defence of the Realm Act (DORA) passed
**Aug/Sept** Battles of Tannenberg and Masurian Lakes on Eastern Front
**Sept** Trench warfare begins on Western Front

**1915**
**Jan** Poison gas first used
**Apr** Gallipoli campaign begins
**Dec** Siege of Kut begins
Munitions crisis

**1916**
**Jan** Conscription introduced
**Feb** Battle for Verdun begins
**May** Battle of Jutland

# WHAT WAS DONE TO MAKE MORE MUNITIONS?

## The shell shortage

The severity of fighting on the Western Front meant that British forces soon began to run out of shells. Reports of the 'shell scandal' filled British newspapers in the spring of 1915: they claimed a lack of shells was causing British military failures on the Western Front.

## Making more munitions

The government responded by creating a Ministry of Munitions to organise munitions production. Led by Lloyd George (the future Prime Minister), it succeeded in increasing the numbers of shells manufactured in Britain from just 500,000 in 1914 to 76.2 million in 1917. It did this by:

- building new munitions factories and encouraging other factories to switch to the production of war materials; for example, bicycle factories became shell factories
- directly managing factories to improve their efficiency
- encouraging more people to work in munitions factories and improving worker efficiency through a variety of incentives and restrictions. These included forcing pubs to close early (by 10 p.m.), adding water to beer and spirits to weaken them, and making strikes illegal in government-controlled factories.

An 'On War Service' badge, issued to those employed in essential war work. Essential war industries included munitions manufacture, coal mining and shipbuilding. Their employees were encouraged *not* to enlist in the army. It was hoped that war service badges would deter people calling them cowards because they were not in army uniform.

**Source A** Lloyd George, Minister of Munitions, speaking to the Shipbuilding Employers Federation, in March 1915.

We are fighting Germans, Austrians and Drink, and so far as I can see the greatest of these deadly foes is Drink.

**Source B** Munitions workers guide six-inch howitzer shells being lowered to the floor at the Chilwell ammunition factory in Nottinghamshire, July 1917.

1917
Feb British re-take Kut
Apr USA joins the War
Jul Battle of Passchendaele begins
Dec Armistice between Russia and Germany

1918
Feb Ration books introduced
Mar German Spring Offensive begins
Nov Armistice

1919
Treaty of Versailles

# Welcoming women workers

By the end of the War, 2.9 million women were employed in the munitions industry, a rise of 800,000 since 1914. The majority were working class. Before the War they would have worked in textile factories, or as maids or nurses. The salary for a female munitions worker was very good compared to these jobs, though they were still paid less than male workers.

Women in work often faced hostility from their male co-workers, many of whom feared that 'cheap' female labour would lead to their own wages being reduced. To reassure the men, the government promised that all women working in formerly 'male' roles would be asked to leave these jobs when the War was over.

Munitions workers were also at risk of **TNT** poisoning, which eventually killed 109 women and made thousands more severely ill. The chemical dyed the skin and hair yellow, earning female munitions workers the nickname 'canary girls'. Explosions were also a hazard in factories making shells. An explosion at the Silvertown TNT factory in East London on 19 January 1917 killed 73, injured 400 and destroyed over 900 homes, with thousands more suffering damage.

## LOTTIE'S STORY

Charlotte 'Lottie' Meade lived in a poor area of London. She had five children, one of whom had died as a baby. She worked in a wartime munitions factory in London. In October 1916 she fell into a coma, suffering from liver, kidney and heart failure. Her death was caused by TNT poisoning as a result of exposure to dangerous chemicals in the factory.
At the time of her death her eldest child was seven and the youngest was just one. Lottie's husband was a soldier in France and did not make it home before she died. He remarried in 1920 to a young widow whose husband had been killed in the War.
In this photograph, Lottie wears the uniform of a female munitions worker. Such overalls would never have been worn by women before the War; dresses and skirts were the norm. She is also wearing the 'On War Service' badge (see page 40).

## ACTIVITY

1. a) Read Lottie's Story above. List what you learn from it about munitions workers during the War.
   b) List the advantages and disadvantages for women working in munitions factories.
2. Read Source C.
   a) What does it tell us about women munitions workers during the War?
   b) What aspects of their behaviour might the author not approve?
3. Design a poster explaining what the Government did to increase munitions production during the War.

**Source C** Madeline Ida Bedford's poem, a **parody** about female munitions workers during the War. She was a middle-class woman who was not a munitions worker.

**Munition Wages**

Earning high wages? Yus,

Five quid a week,

A woman, too, mind you,

I calls it dim sweet.

Ye'are asking some questions –

But bless yer, here goes:

I spends the whole racket

On good times and clothes.

… We're all here today, mate,

Tomorrow – perhaps dead,

If Fate tumbles on us

And blows up our shed.

Afraid! Are yer kidding?

With money to spend!

Years back I wore tatters,

Now – silk stockings, mi friend!

I've bracelets and jewellery,

Rings envied by friends,

A sergeant to swank with,

And something to lend.

I drive out in taxis,

Do theatres in style,

And this is my verdict –

It is jolly worthwhile.

**1914**
Aug War begins
Aug Defence of the Realm Act (DORA) passed
Aug/Sept Battles of Tannenberg and Masurian Lakes on Eastern Front
Sept Trench warfare begins on Western Front

**1915**
Jan Poison gas first used
Apr Gallipoli campaign begins
Dec Siege of Kut begins
Munitions crisis

**1916**
Jan Conscription introduced
Feb Battle for Verdun begins
May Battle of Jutland
Jul Battle of the Somme begins

# HOW WELL DID BRITAIN FEED ITSELF DURING THE WAR?

As well as making sure there were enough munitions during the War, the government had to make sure people had enough food to eat.

## Why were there food shortages in Britain?

Britain relied on **imports** for about 60 per cent of all food before the War. German U-boats began torpedoing **merchant ships** carrying food supplies to Britain, causing food shortages. Shipping losses were at their worst in 1917, when in April alone over 500,000 tonnes of British merchant shipping was sunk. Shortages were made worse by widespread hoarding, and increasing food prices, especially for scarce items like wheat products, meat and eggs.

To prevent food shortages becoming severe the government took measures to increase imports, increase food production and ensure the fair distribution of available food to the population.

## Protecting merchant ships

The introduction of the **convoy system** in May 1917 was hugely successful in reducing the number of merchant ships sunk by U-boats. In the convoy system, merchant ships sailed together in large groups, rather than as individual ships. Convoys were usually given the protection of a naval battleship destroyer for part of their voyage.

## Increasing food production

To grow more food, the government did the following:
- Turned parks and unused land into allotments for growing food. The King even had the flowerbeds at Buckingham Palace converted to vegetable patches.
- Instructed farmers to use more land for growing crops.
- Exempted agricultural workers from conscription.
- Encouraged women to help in farming work.

These measures worked but only increased food supplies by a small amount. The government therefore looked for another way to help stop food shortages – controlling consumption.

**Source A** Joe Hollister, a Londoner, writing in a letter to his father in Essex on 19 March 1917.

We want to find [ways] to deal effectively with [German] submarines to relieve the scarcity of food stuffs … things in London in this respect are beginning to be serious, no potatoes to be had, sugar almost unobtainable, meat and cheese, butter and bread [all at high prices]. I tried vegetables instead of flowers in the garden last year, not that I expected much, more from patriotic motives, beans, [cabbages], sprouts, lettuce, onions, carrots, but it was just a waste of money and time and so disheartening and so I think I shall just keep it tidy this year and no more.

▲ **Source B** A poster encouraging people to avoid wasting food.

1917
Feb British re-take Kut
Apr USA joins the War
Jul Battle of Passchendaele begins
Dec Armistice between Russia and Germany

1918
Feb Ration books introduced
Mar German Spring Offensive begins
Nov Armistice

1919
Treaty of Versailles

# Rationing

At first, the government was reluctant to force people to restrict their food intake. Instead, they encouraged people to eat less, have 'meatless days' and avoid food waste (see Sources B and C).

As shortages worsened, the government took more direct action: rationing. This was first introduced February 1918. A ration book was issued to everyone, including the King.

Bread was considered such a basic necessity that it was not rationed, and instead the government fixed the price at 9 pence. It wasn't all good news though, as wheat flour was increasingly replaced by alternatives like potato flour, resulting in a dark, unpleasant loaf.

**The weekly ration was fixed at:**

| | |
|---|---|
| | Beef, mutton or lamb, 15oz (425g) – the equivalent of four quarterpounder burgers. |
| | Bacon, 5oz (140g) – about five slices. |
| Fats, 4oz (113g) – half a packet of butter or margarine. | Sugar, 8oz (225g) – half a typical bag of sugar. |

▲ The weekly amounts of rationed goods from 1918.

# Did the government do enough?

Despite the food shortages, the average calorific intake only fell by 3 per cent during the war years compared to 1914. People's diets were certainly different, but government measures helped to ensure that, at least in Britain, deprivation never threatened to become starvation.

## MR SLICE O'BREAD

I am a slice of bread …

I am wasted everyday by 48,000,000 people of Britain.

I am the 'bit left over', the slice eaten absent-mindedly when I really wasn't needed; I am the waste crust.

If you collected me and my companions for a whole week you would find that we amounted to 9,380 tonnes of good bread – WASTED!

Two shiploads of good bread.

Almost as much as 20 German submarines … could sink even if they had good luck.

When you throw me away or waste me, you are adding 20 submarines to the German Navy!

▲ **Source C** Ministry of Food leaflet produced by the government, July 1917.

### ACTIVITY

1. Why were there food shortages in Britain during the War?
2. a) To what extent do Sources B and C present a similar message? Refer to the Sources in your answer.
   b) Do you think Source B or Source C is more effective in presenting its message? Give reasons for your answer.
3. Design an information leaflet produced by the government in 1917 to instruct people about:
   a) why there is a need to save food; and
   b) what they can do to help prevent food shortages.

**1914**
Aug War begins
Aug Defence of the Realm Act (DORA) passed
Aug/Sept Battles of Tannenberg and Masurian Lakes on Eastern Front
Sept Trench warfare begins on Western Front

**1915**
Jan Poison gas first used
Apr Gallipoli campaign begins
Dec Siege of Kut begins
Munitions crisis

**1916**
Jan Conscription introduced
Feb Battle for Verdun begins
May Battle of Jutland
Jul Battle of the Somme begins

# WAS ANYONE WINNING THE WAR ON THE WESTERN FRONT IN 1917?

By early 1917, German troops in France had withdrawn to the **Hindenburg Line**, a particularly strong series of trenches. This made it even harder for the Allies to break the stalemate. Nevertheless the Allies launched attacks throughout 1917 to try to force an end to the War (see map below).

▼ The Allied attacks in 1917.

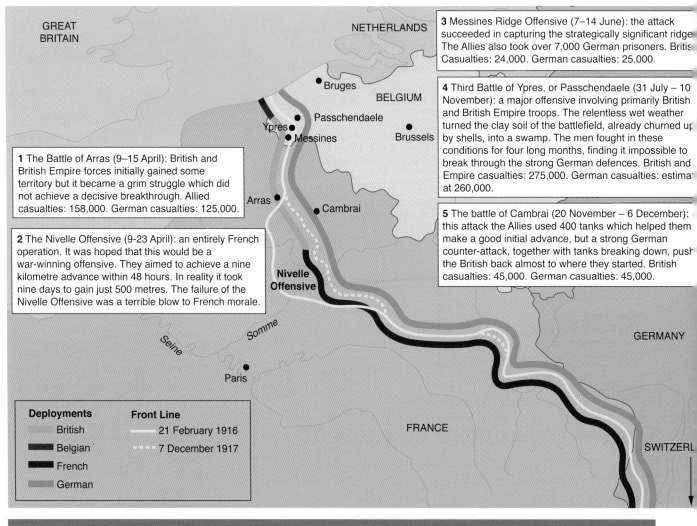

**3** Messines Ridge Offensive (7–14 June): the attack succeeded in capturing the strategically significant ridge. The Allies also took over 7,000 German prisoners. British Casualties: 24,000. German casualties: 25,000.

**4** Third Battle of Ypres, or Passchendaele (31 July – 10 November): a major offensive involving primarily British and British Empire troops. The relentless wet weather turned the clay soil of the battlefield, already churned up by shells, into a swamp. The men fought in these conditions for four long months, finding it impossible to break through the strong German defences. British and Empire casualties: 275,000. German casualties: estimated at 260,000.

**1** The Battle of Arras (9–15 April): British and British Empire forces initially gained some territory but it became a grim struggle which did not achieve a decisive breakthrough. Allied casualties: 158,000. German casualties: 125,000.

**5** The battle of Cambrai (20 November – 6 December): this attack the Allies used 400 tanks which helped them make a good initial advance, but a strong German counter-attack, together with tanks breaking down, pushed the British back almost to where they started. British casualties: 45,000. German casualties: 45,000.

**2** The Nivelle Offensive (9-23 April): an entirely French operation. It was hoped that this would be a war-winning offensive. They aimed to achieve a nine kilometre advance within 48 hours. In reality it took nine days to gain just 500 metres. The failure of the Nivelle Offensive was a terrible blow to French morale.

| Deployments | Front Line |
|---|---|
| British | ——— 21 February 1916 |
| Belgian | - - - - 7 December 1917 |
| French | |
| German | |

## THE SEABROOKS' STORY

The Australian brothers, Theo, William (known as Keith) and George Seabrook, enlisted together in August 1916. They were all killed at Passchendaele on 20 September 1917 (see page 44). It was their first attack. The two elder brothers, Theo (25) and George (24), were probably killed by the same shell. Their bodies were never found. The youngest, Keith (21), was fatally wounded and died the next day. The news of the brothers' deaths devastated their family. Their father suffered a mental breakdown and lost his job, forcing the family to sell their home. Their mother continued to hope that George, who was never officially confirmed dead during the War, had somehow survived.

**1917**
**Feb** British re-take Kut
**Apr** USA joins the War
**Jul** Battle of Passchendaele begins
**Dec** Armistice between Russia and Germany

**1918**
**Feb** Ration books introduced
**Mar** German Spring Offensive begins
**Nov** Armistice

**1919**
Treaty of Versailles

The Allies faced other problems in 1917:

- Large sections of the French Army **mutinied**; around 60 per cent of French troops on the Western Front refused to obey orders to move into front line trenches and demanded peace. The mutinies, however, did not last long.
- Russia was regularly losing 200,000 men each month by 1916, and there were extreme food shortages for civilians on the home front. **Communist** revolutionaries seized power in Russia in November 1917 and asked the German government for an **armistice**. This meant that Russia would withdraw from the War and thousands of German troops might be transferred from the Eastern to the Western Front.

# Signs of hope?

None of the Allied offensives in 1917 achieved a major breakthrough, but they had caused serious casualties to the Germans. The Germans could not sustain these losses – crucially, the Allies could fight for longer because:

- The Allies had a larger pool of reserves (they could enlist people from the vast British Empire to fight).
- Thousands of US troops were on their way to help the Allies. The USA declared war on Germany on 6 April 1917, in part because Germany had been sinking US ships which had been providing supplies to Britain. The first US troops arrived in June 1917, though they would not reach the Western Front until May 1918.
- The civilian populations in Germany, Austria–Hungary and Turkey were suffering extreme shortages and hardships (see pages 46–47).

**ACTIVITY**

1. Look at the map on page 44.
   a) What aspects of the Allied offensives in 1917 did not go well for the Allies?
   b) The Allied offensives were not all failures. What aspects could be seen as positive for the Allies?
2. a) What impression does Source A give of a battlefield? Give examples from the painting in your answer.
   b) How reliable is this painting as evidence of what battlefields were like during the Battle of Passchendaele?
3. Find evidence to support each of the statements:
   'In 1917 it looks like the Allies are going to lose the War.'
   'In 1917 it seems the Allies are going to win the War.'

▲ **Source A** *The Menin Road*, a painting by the official British war artist, Paul Nash, 1919. The painting was based on scenes of the War the artist had observed in Belgium. It was originally commissioned to hang in a Hall of Remembrance in 1919 that was never built. Nash wrote to his wife Margaret in November 1917 of what he had seen at Passchendaele: 'The rain drives on, the stinking mud becomes more evilly yellow, the shell holes fill up with green-white water, the roads and tracks are covered in inches of slime, the black dying trees ooze and sweat and the shells never cease.'

| 1914 | 1915 | 1916 |
|------|------|------|
| **Aug** War begins | **Jan** Poison gas first used | **Jan** Conscription introduced |
| **Aug** Defence of the Realm Act (DORA) passed | **Apr** Gallipoli campaign begins | **Feb** Battle for Verdun begins |
| **Aug/Sept** Battles of Tannenberg and Masurian Lakes on Eastern Front | **Dec** Siege of Kut begins | **May** Battle of Jutland |
| **Sept** Trench warfare begins on Western Front | Munitions crisis | **Jul** Battle of the Somme begins |

# HOW MUCH LONGER COULD GERMANY HANG ON?

By the beginning of 1918, Germany and its allies were suffering heavily from shortages of men for their armies, and supplies to feed their civilians.

## A lack of reserves

After nearly four years of war, the German Army had used almost all of its reserves of manpower. Without a large empire from which to draw men, the army was forced to conscript the very young, the middle aged and the less fit. In the final months of the War, tens of thousands of men, many just seventeen years old, were sent to the Front. These new troops entered the War with low morale because they knew how badly Germany was suffering at home, and there were cases of soldiers getting drunk and even looting.

**Source A** The German writer, Rudolf Binding, who at the age of 46 became a commander on the Western Front, writing in his diary in the spring of 1918.

Today the advance of our infantry suddenly stopped. Nobody could understand why. Our airmen had reported no enemy … our way seemed clear. [I saw one of our men] carrying a hen under one arm and a box of notepaper under the other. [Another] was carrying a bottle of wine with another one open in their hand. Evidently [many] had found it desirable to loot …

▼ **Source B** German soldiers guarding a looted butcher's shop in Berlin in 1918. The neighbouring chemist and bookshop have not been plundered.

**1917**
Feb British re-take Kut
Apr USA joins the War
Jul Battle of Passchendaele begins
Dec Armistice between Russia and Germany

**1918**
Feb Ration books introduced
Mar German Spring Offensive begins
Nov Armistice

**1919**
Treaty of Versailles

# A lack of supplies

Food shortages had become severe in Germany by 1918. This was partly the result of the Allied naval blockade that had been in place since 1914, which prevented food supplies entering German ports.

Rationing was established in 1915 for essential food stuffs, and provided for less than 2,000 calories per person per day. In reality, Germans ate even less than this as many items were often simply not available. The failure of the 1916 potato harvest made people depend on beet vegetables, like turnips, normally used as animal feed. By 1918, thousands relied on soup kitchens to stave off starvation. The daily bread ration was down to only a quarter of a loaf and milk was almost impossible to find.

Some people turned to looting in desperation, as Source B shows. To try to help, the government introduced food substitutes ('ersatz' foods). They eventually licensed over 11,000 ersatz products (see table below).

| PRODUCT | MADE FROM ... |
|---------|---------------|
| Meat | Pressed rice, mushrooms boiled in mutton fat and sometimes even finished off with a fake bone made of wood. |
| Bread | Flour, potatoes, beans, peas and buckwheat; usually barely edible. |
| Coffee | Dandelion roots and barley. |
| Tea | Strawberry or raspberry leaves. |
| Cocoa | Roasted peas, rye and chemical flavouring. |

▲ Ersatz foods.

# Germany's suffering and unrest

**Malnutrition** affected many Germans and thousands, weakened by hunger, succumbed to diseases like tuberculosis, influenza and pneumonia. As many as 762,000 German civilians died from malnutrition and associated diseases.

Socialist-inspired demonstrations, which demanded better living and working conditions, grew popular as more and more people suffered. In Berlin in January 1918, half a million workers went on strike. Such action had a damaging impact on the war effort, and showed that Germany could not keep going with the War much longer – it was causing too much unrest at home.

## What about Germany's allies?

Germany's main allies, Austria–Hungary, Turkey and Bulgaria, all seemed to be nearing collapse by the beginning of 1918. Their civilian populations were badly affected by food shortages and they were suffering military defeats on the battlefield. If Germany's allies collapsed, then Germany's war would be lost.

If Germany could act to end the War quickly and triumph with one last massive assault then, perhaps, just perhaps, they might win.

**Source C** Elfriede Kuhr, a German teenager, working in children's hospital in Schneidemühl, writing in her diary in 1918. Many of the children in the hospital were suffering from malnutrition and had been handed in by their mothers; soldiers' wives no longer able to cope.

Oh, these babies! Just skin and bone. Little starving bodies … when they cry it is no louder than a weak little whimper. There is a little boy who is bound to die soon. He has a face like a dried-up mummy … he is only six months old.

## ACTIVITY

1. a) List five examples that show there were food shortages in Germany by 1918.
   b) What impact did the food shortages begin to have on civilians in Germany?
2. What evidence was there that the German Army was being weakened by the impact of shortages?
3. a) Make a copy of the continuum below. Shade it in to show how much longer you think Germany could hold on by the beginning of 1918 before surrendering or being defeated.
   By the beginning of 1918 Germany could hold on:

   just days — months — years

   b) Explain your decision.

**1914**
Aug War begins
Aug Defence of the Realm Act (DORA) passed
Aug/Sept Battles of Tannenberg and Masurian Lakes on Eastern Front
Sept Trench warfare begins on Western Front

**1915**
Jan Poison gas first used
Apr Gallipoli campaign begins
Dec Siege of Kut begins
Munitions crisis

**1916**
Jan Conscription introduced
Feb Battle for Verdun begins
May Battle of Jutland
Jul Battle of the Somme begins

# WHY DID GERMANY'S FINAL GAMBLE GO WRONG?

Time was running out for a German victory by 1918. The leading German general, Erich Ludendorff, planned a series of massive assaults on the Western Front to begin on 21 March 1918. This was Germany's last gamble for victory.

The German Spring Offensives, as they became known, were initially very successful. By early June German troops in some places had advanced over 70 kilometres. A new phase of mobile war as opposed to trench warfare had begun, and the Allies were in retreat.

Such a big advance was achieved by the German use of highly trained assault troops and immense artillery bombardment to begin the attacks. The assault troops invaded the weakest points of the Allied trenches to disrupt the Allied defensive line from within.

But by July 1918, the German advance had begun to slow. The reasons for this are shown on the map above.

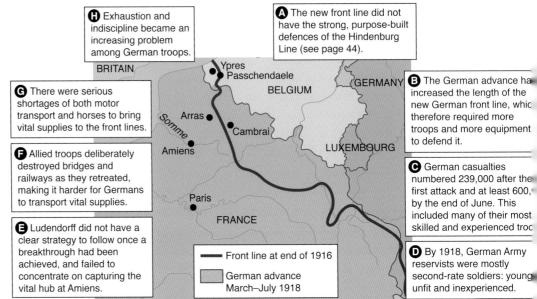

**H** Exhaustion and indiscipline became an increasing problem among German troops.

**A** The new front line did not have the strong, purpose-built defences of the Hindenburg Line (see page 44).

**G** There were serious shortages of both motor transport and horses to bring vital supplies to the front lines.

**B** The German advance ha[s] increased the length of the new German front line, whic[h] therefore required more troops and more equipment to defend it.

**F** Allied troops deliberately destroyed bridges and railways as they retreated, making it harder for Germans to transport vital supplies.

**C** German casualties numbered 239,000 after the first attack and at least 600,[000] by the end of June. This included many of their most skilled and experienced troo[ps].

**E** Ludendorff did not have a clear strategy to follow once a breakthrough had been achieved, and failed to concentrate on capturing the vital hub at Amiens.

**D** By 1918, German Army reservists were mostly second-rate soldiers: young, unfit and inexperienced.

Front line at end of 1916

German advance March–July 1918

BRITAIN

Ypres
Passchendaele

BELGIUM

GERMANY

Arras

Somme

Cambrai

Amiens

LUXEMBOURG

Paris

FRANCE

▲ The extent of the German advance on the Western Front from March to July 1918.

▼ **Source A** German supply wagons struggling across rough, clogged roads in March 1918.

1917
Feb British re-take Kut
Apr USA joins the War
Jul Battle of Passchendaele begins
Dec Armistice between Russia and Germany

1918
Feb Ration books introduced
Mar German Spring Offensive begins
Nov Armistice

1919
Treaty of Versailles

**GEORGE'S STORY**

George Doman, born near Bolton in Lancashire, was 17 when war broke out. At the age of 21 he was fighting in France and was wounded in both legs on the first day of the German Spring Offensives. He was then taken prisoner and sent back to Germany as a prisoner of war (**PoW**). He was one of 90,000 British prisoners taken during the rapid German advance. About 160,000 British soldiers became prisoners during the War. Doman was sent to eastern Germany. He died there on 11 June 1918. He is buried in Poznan Garrison Cemetery, in what is now Poland.

# The Allied counter-attacks

The Allies launched major counter-attacks against the Germans from August 1918. By September 1918, they had regained the ground lost during the Spring Offensives. They then pushed the German troops back further, breaking through the Hindenburg Line in late September.

The Allies benefited enormously from the influx of US troops, which by September numbered over 1.7 million men in Europe. They fought alongside British and French troops in the counter-attacks of 1918. American casualties in these last months of the War were high.

With the Hindenburg Line broken and German troops repeatedly in retreat, it was clear that Germany was losing the War.

**Source B** Sergeant Melvin Krulewitch from the United States Marine Corps recalling after the War his part in an attack on the Western Front in November 1918.

On we moved … [our] artillery fire had almost wiped out the first row of [German] trenches so we were soon in them and taking prisoners. The Germans were losing their food; losing their artillery horses and their baggage and ration wagons. They were so hungry they would shoot a horse and cut steaks out of it.

**Source C** Erich Maria Remarque, a German soldier during the First World War, writing in his novel *All Quiet on the Western Front*, 1928.

Our lines are falling back. There are too many fresh English and American regiments … But we are emaciated and starved. Our food is bad and mixed up with so much substitute stuff that it makes us ill … Our artillery is fired out, it has too few shells … we have too few horses. Our fresh troops are anaemic boys in need of rest, who cannot carry a pack, but merely know how to die.

**ACTIVITY**

1.  a)  Using the information on page 48, list eight reasons why the German Spring Offensives failed.
    b)  Colour code your list of reasons to show how they fit into the following categories:
        * issues of supply
        * issues of strategy
        * issues of morale
        * issues of strength/numbers of troops.
2.  a)  How far do Sources B and C agree about the reasons for the retreat of the German troops?
    b)  How reliable are Sources B and C in understanding the retreat of the German troops?

▲ **Source D** US troops playing a dice game at Camp Flower Down, Winchester, England (1918).

1914
Aug War begins
Aug Defence of the Realm Act (DORA) passed
Aug/Sept Battles of Tannenberg and Masurian Lakes on Eastern Front
Sept Trench warfare begins on Western Front

1915
Jan Poison gas first used
Apr Gallipoli campaign begins
Dec Siege of Kut begins
Munitions crisis

1916
Jan Conscription introduced
Feb Battle for Verdun begins
May Battle of Jutland
Jul Battle of the Somme begins

# HOW WAS PEACE MADE?

By the autumn of 1918 the German situation looked hopeless:

- The Spring Offensives had failed.
- Germany's allies had collapsed; Bulgaria and Turkey stopped fighting in late October 1918, Austria–Hungary on 3 November 1918.
- German troops were deserting in increased numbers.
- Hardships for German civilians worsened and there were growing demands for peace.
- Socialist demonstrations increased in Germany. This worried Germany's wealthy ruling classes, who wanted a quick end to the War in order to focus on putting down these revolutionary protests.

Germany's leader, Kaiser Wilhelm II, finally accepted the German generals' advice that an armistice was necessary. He then left Germany for neutral Holland on 10 November 1918.

## The Armistice

The Armistice was signed on 11 November 1918. As a result Germany agreed to:

- remove all of its troops from Belgium and France within fifteen days
- remove all troops from territories in what had been the Eastern Front
- cancel the **Treaty of Brest-Litovsk**
- repatriate all prisoners and deported civilians
- give up most of their weapons of War, including almost all their artillery, 25,000 machine guns, 1,700 aeroplanes, 5,000 railway engines, 10 battleships, all their submarines, and all their military aircraft
- pay for all damage done and repairs needed in Belgium and France.

A souvenir replica key from the railway carriage at Compiègne in northern France where the Armistice was signed. The signing took place at 5:10 a.m. on 11 November 1918 and became active at 11 a.m. – the eleventh hour of the eleventh day of the eleventh month. This key was made into a tie-clip and sold to tourists visiting the historic railway carriage.

**Source A** Colonel Thomas Gowenlock, an intelligence officer in the American 1st Army Division on the front line, recalling his memories of the Armistice in the book *Soldiers of Darkness* in 1936.

'One the morning of November 11, I [was] sat in my dugout [when] a signal corps officer entered and handed us the following message ... hostilities will be stopped on the entire front beginning at 11 o'clock.' ... My watch said nine o'clock. With only two hours to go, I drove [to the front line] to see the finish. The shelling was heavy and, as I walked down the road, it grew steadily worse. It seemed to me that every battery [gun] in the world was trying to burn up its guns. At last eleven o'clock came – but the firing continued. The men on both sides had decided to give each other all they had – their farewell to arms. It was a very natural impulse after their years of war, but unfortunately many fell after eleven o'clock that day.'

**Source B** British soldier, Corporal Reginald Haine, remembering reactions to the Armistice.

It wasn't like London, where they all got drunk of course. No, it wasn't like that, it was all very quiet. You were so dazed you just didn't realise that you could stand up straight and not be shot.

**Source C** The British newspaper, the *Daily Mirror*, reporting on the Armistice celebrations in London, 12 November 1918.

**Wonderful Scenes of Enthusiasm Everywhere – City Given Up to Rejoicings**

London went wild with delight when the great news came through yesterday. Bells burst forth into joyful chimes ... bands paraded the streets followed by cheering crowds of soldiers and civilians and London generally gave itself up wholeheartedly to rejoicing.

1917
Feb British re-take Kut
Apr USA joins the War
Jul Battle of Passchendaele begins
Dec Armistice between Russia and Germany

1918
Feb Ration books introduced
Mar German Spring Offensive begins
Nov Armistice

1919
Treaty of Versailles

# Reactions to the Armistice

News of the Armistice was greeted with euphoria and relief as well as with enormous sadness at what had been lost in the struggle to achieve peace.

In many of the defeated countries, the end of the War was far from peaceful. Revolutionary uprisings occurred in Germany in January 1919 as communists attempted, but ultimately failed, to seize power. The Austro-Hungarian Empire fell apart as different ethnic groups proclaimed their independence.

The enormous and difficult task of trying to make a lasting peace out of the ruins of war fell to the politicians of the victorious countries. They met at peace conferences in 1919 to decide the exact details of how the defeated countries were going to pay for the War.

> **ACTIVITY**
>
> 1. a) Which do you consider to be the three most severe Armistice terms for Germany? Give reasons for your answer.
>    b) Why did Germany accept such vague, harsh Armistice terms?
> 2. Compare Sources A, B, C and D showing reactions to the Armistice.
>    a) What are the similarities and differences between the Sources?
>    b) How can you explain the differences?

▼ **Source D** People celebrating the Armistice in London riding inside a US automobile.

**1914**
Aug War begins
Aug Defence of the Realm Act (DORA) passed
Aug/Sept Battles of Tannenberg and Masurian Lakes on Eastern Front
Sept Trench warfare begins on Western Front

**1915**
Jan Poison gas first used
Apr Gallipoli campaign begins
Dec Siege of Kut begins
    Munitions crisis

**1916**
Jan Conscription introduced
Feb Battle for Verdun begins
May Battle of Jutland
Jul Battle of the Somme begins

# WHAT WAS THE COST OF THE WAR?

It is impossible to calculate the true cost of the War. With nearly 10 million military dead alone, it was the most deadly European conflict that history had yet seen. But there were losses the statistics do not show – the losses felt by orphans, widows, hopeful brides; all those affected by the lives that were never lived because of the War.

## The human cost

The military dead from all sides was enormous.

In addition, almost 22 million men were wounded – psychologically and physically. Many soldiers suffered from 'shell shock', the symptoms of which included anxiety, nervous tics and severe nightmares. Hundreds of thousands of men struggled with disabilities: the loss of limbs, blindness and deafness. Many found it very difficult to find work after the War or help for their condition.

## Civilian deaths

It is hard to know the exact number of civilian casualties caused by the War. In Britain there were just over 1,500 civilian deaths, in France over 40,000, and in Germany up to 425,000. The numbers of people dying from disease were also higher than average; the deadly flu pandemic of 1918–1919 killed an estimated 21 million people worldwide.

▲ **Source A** A poster produced by the Labour Party encouraging people to vote Labour in the 1918 general election. It criticises the lack of help the government provided to returning soldiers, many of whom struggled find work, cope with their injuries and what they had experienced during the War.

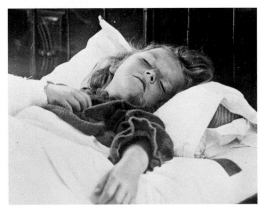

▲ **Source B** British schoolgirl, Betty Constance, in hospital suffering from injuries to her legs and arms caused by a German zeppelin raid on Southend in November 1917. Zeppelin raids caused 1,413 deaths in Britain during the War.

| COUNTRY | NUMBERS OF TROOPS KILLED | PERCENTAGE KILLED OF MEN WHO SERVED |
|---|---|---|
| Russia | 1,800,000 | 15 |
| Serbia | 275,000 | 37 |
| France | 1,390,000 | 16 |
| Britain and British Empire | 1,000,000 | 10 |
| Italy | 460,000 | 7 |
| USA | 50,000 | 1 |
| Germany | 2,040,000 | 15 |
| Austria–Hungary | 1,020,000 | 13 |
| Turkey | 240,000 | 24 |

▲ The numbers of military dead.

**1917**
Feb British re-take Kut
Apr USA joins the War
Jul Battle of Passchendaele begins
Dec Armistice between Russia and Germany

**1918**
Feb Ration books introduced
Mar German Spring Offensive begins
Nov Armistice

**1919**
Treaty of Versailles

# The economic cost

All European countries spent huge amounts of money during the War. The Allied countries together spent an estimated $147 billion, the Central Powers $208.5 billion. Almost all ended the War in debt (mainly to the USA). Serious **inflation** meant economic hardships for ordinary people. The price of most foods more than doubled in Britain during the War, with some like mutton and sugar tripling in price.

Many countries suffered destruction to their land, towns and industries that would have to be repaired. Vast swathes of territory in the Russian Empire were laid to waste. In France, estimates suggest 21,000 square kilometres of land (the size of Wales) was seriously damaged.

> **ACTIVITY**
> 1. a) List in order the five countries from which most men died during the War.
>    b) List in order the five countries which had the highest percentage killed of men who served.
> 2. Lots of soldiers died in the War, but what were the other human costs of the War, for soldiers and civilians?
> 3. List the economic costs of the War.

**Source C** The ruins of the historic city of Ypres in Belgium. It would need to be completely rebuilt after the War.

**1914**
Aug War begins
Aug Defence of the Realm Act (DORA) passed
Aug/Sept Battles of Tannenberg and Masurian Lakes on Eastern Front
Sept Trench warfare begins on Western Front

**1915**
Jan Poison gas first used
Apr Gallipoli campaign begins
Dec Siege of Kut begins
Munitions crisis

**1916**
Jan Conscription introduced
Feb Battle for Verdun begins
May Battle of Jutland
Jul Battle of the Somme begins

# HOW WAS GERMANY PUNISHED BY THE TREATY OF VERSAILLES?

Thirty countries sent representatives to the peace talks, but the discussions were dominated by the 'Big Three': the leaders of France (Georges Clemenceau), Britain (David Lloyd George) and the United States (Woodrow Wilson). The peace talks would have to deal with many difficult issues including:

- who was to pay for the damage caused by the War, and how much,
- where new borders between countries should be drawn,
- how best to try to prevent war from breaking out in the future.

The leaders disagreed about how harshly Germany should be treated. Clemenceau felt their aims would be best achieved by a treaty that punished Germany, whilst Woodrow Wilson sought something less severe, which would be based on the Fourteen Points for peace that he had drawn up during the War. These included the establishment of a League of Nations. This was an organisation of representatives from nations that would work together to improve health, living and working conditions throughout the world as well as to provide arbitration between countries in an attempt to prevent disagreements escalating to war.

The main terms of the Treaty of Versailles are shown below. Opinion was divided about whether the Treaty was fair; some criticised it as too harsh, others as not harsh enough.

▼ The leaders meeting in Paris for the peace talks. From left to right: Vittorio Orlando, the Italian Prime Minister, David Lloyd George, Georges Clemenceau, Woodrow Wilson.

**1917**
Feb British re-take Kut
Apr USA joins the War
Jul Battle of Passchendaele begins
Dec Armistice between Russia and Germany

**1918**
Feb Ration books introduced
Mar German Spring Offensive begins
Nov Armistice

**1919**
Treaty of Versailles

**Blame**
Germany had to accept the 'war guilt clause' – that Germany and its allies were fully responsible for causing the War as well as for all the loss and damage that resulted. This caused huge resentment among Germans who had been told that they were fighting a defensive war.

Germany, and the other defeated countries, were not permitted to join the League of Nations.

▼ The terms of the Treaty of Versailles (1919).

**Reparations**
The Allies set the amount of reparations to be paid by Germany at $33 billion (£6.6 billion or 132 billion German marks) in 1921. This was to be paid over 42 years. The majority (52%) was to go to France.

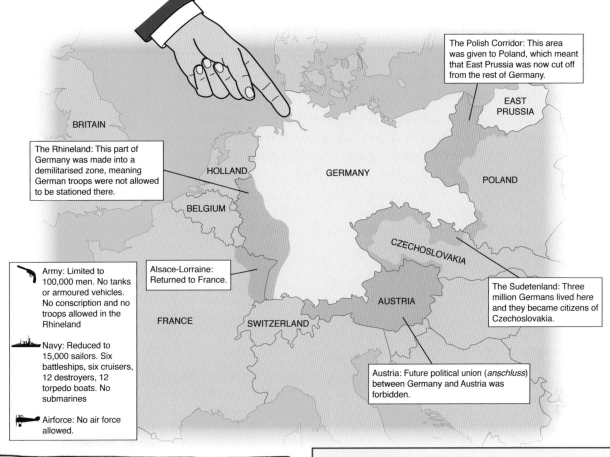

The Polish Corridor: This area was given to Poland, which meant that East Prussia was now cut off from the rest of Germany.

EAST PRUSSIA

BRITAIN

The Rhineland: This part of Germany was made into a demilitarised zone, meaning German troops were not allowed to be stationed there.

HOLLAND

GERMANY

POLAND

BELGIUM

CZECHOSLOVAKIA

Army: Limited to 100,000 men. No tanks or armoured vehicles. No conscription and no troops allowed in the Rhineland

Alsace-Lorraine: Returned to France.

AUSTRIA

The Sudetenland: Three million Germans lived here and they became citizens of Czechoslovakia.

FRANCE          SWITZERLAND

Navy: Reduced to 15,000 sailors. Six battleships, six cruisers, 12 destroyers, 12 torpedo boats. No submarines

Austria: Future political union (*anschluss*) between Germany and Austria was forbidden.

Airforce: No air force allowed.

DER TAG!

▲ **Source A** A political cartoon, published in Britain in 1919, by David Low: 'A bitter pill to swallow'. The figure on the right represents Germany, being force-fed a pill by the Allied leaders from left to right: Lloyd George (Britain), Vittorio Orlando (Italy), Georges Clemenceau (France) and Woodrow Wilson (USA).

## ACTIVITY

1. Which specific terms of the Treaty of Versailles dealt with each of the following aims? Try to give one or two examples for each.
   a) Ensure Germany couldn't attack in the future.
   b) Seek reparations for the damage caused by the War and help with war debts.
   c) Decide on borders and territories.
2. Germany was punished by the treaty. Which of the terms do you think might have been seen as the harshest and least justifiable by Germany? Give reasons for your choices.
3. a) Explain what is happening in the cartoon.
   b) What do you think the cartoonist thought of the Treaty of Versailles? Give reasons for your answer.

| 1914 | | 1915 | | 1916 |
|------|--|------|--|------|
| **Aug** War begins | | **Jan** Poison gas first used | | **Jan** Conscription introduced |
| **Aug** Defence of the Realm Act (DORA) passed | | **Apr** Gallipoli campaign begins | | **Feb** Battle for Verdun begins |
| **Aug/Sept** Battles of Tannenberg and Masurian Lakes on Eastern Front | | **Dec** Siege of Kut begins | | **May** Battle of Jutland |
| **Sept** Trench warfare begins on Western Front | | Munitions crisis | | **Jul** Battle of the Somme begins |

# HOW DID THE WAR CHANGE THE WORLD MAP?

The map of Europe looked quite different in 1923 compared to how it had looked in 1914 (see maps below). This was as a result both of the War itself and the peace settlements that were imposed on all the defeated nations after the War.

New borders were drawn in Europe with the defeated nations often losing substantial amounts of land. This was partly along ethnic lines as the post-war peace treaties attempted to create a map of Europe in which peoples of the same ethnic origin were given the opportunity to rule themselves as independent nations, rather than being ruled by huge empires which had been the case before the War.

This was seen in the recognition the peace treaties gave to the new nation of Czechoslovakia, which had been formed in the final months of the War as Czech and Slovak regions broke away from the crumbling control of the Austro-Hungarian Empire. Yugoslavia was formed immediately after the War by the merging of former Austro-Hungarian territories with the Kingdom of Serbia. The Austro-Hungarian Empire broke apart entirely in the final weeks of the War with Hungary declaring its independence just days before the War ended. The Ottoman Empire too ceased to exist, replaced by Turkey which was much smaller.

▲ Europe in 1914. Neth.=Netherlands, Bel.=Belgium, Lux.=Luxembourg, Mont.=Montenegro, Alb.=Albania.

▲ Europe in 1923. Saar=a region of Germany occupied and governed by the UK and France.
Danzig=Free city of German people under control of the League of Nations.

**1917**
Feb British re-take Kut
Apr USA joins the War
Jul Battle of Passchendaele begins
Dec Armistice between Russia and Germany

**1918**
Feb Ration books introduced
Mar German Spring Offensive begins
Nov Armistice

**1919**
Treaty of Versailles

# The Middle East

In the Middle East the First World War left another difficult legacy. The way in which Allies redefined the borders after the collapse of the Ottoman Empire in 1918 (see maps on the right) left the Arabs feeling betrayed. Key territories became British and French **mandates** despite British wartime promises to promote independent Arab rule in return for Arab military help against the Ottoman Empire. This left a legacy of resentment and unrest.

Tensions also worsened between Arabs and Jews over the Allied treatment of Palestine. Palestine became a British mandate after the War and the British government encouraged Jewish immigration to Palestine. Many Jews regarded Palestine as their spiritual homeland and it was already home to some 90,000 Jews by 1918. However, the vast majority of the population was Arab and increased Jewish immigration led to tensions between them. These tensions continue to this day and Palestine remains a bitterly disputed territory.

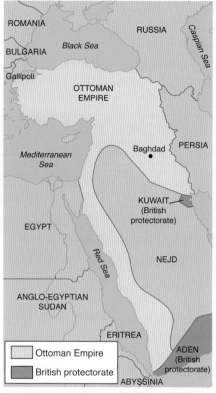

▲ The Middle East in 1914.

## ACTIVITY

1.  a) Identify 5 differences between the map of Europe in 1914 compared to Europe in 1923.
    b) Explain why some of these changes were made to the borders in Europe?
2.  a) Identify 5 differences between the maps of the Middle East before and after the War.
    b) Explain how the First World War worsened problems in the Middle East.
3.  Imagine you are creating a display for an exhibition on the First World War that can use six of the objects from this book.
    a) Select the six objects from the book you would like to include in your exhibition.
    b) Write brief captions for each object explaining:
        ● what the object is,
        ● what the object tells us about the War,
        ● why you chose to include this object.

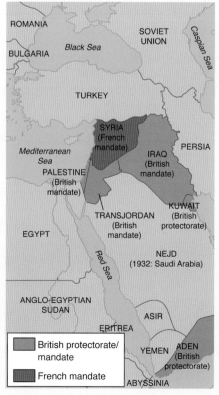

▲ The Middle East in 1923.

| 1914 | 1915 | 1916 |
|---|---|---|
| **Aug** War begins | **Jan** Poison gas first used | **Jan** Conscription introduced |
| **Aug** Defence of the Realm Act (DORA) passed | **Apr** Gallipoli campaign begins | **Feb** Battle for Verdun begins |
| **Aug/Sept** Battles of Tannenberg and Masurian Lakes on Eastern Front | **Dec** Siege of Kut begins | **May** Battle of Jutland |
| **Sept** Trench warfare begins on Western Front | Munitions crisis | **Jul** Battle of the Somme begins |

# HOW WAS THE WAR REMEMBERED?

The First World War has been widely remembered in art, literature, sculpture and memorials throughout the world. These help to ensure that people's experiences of the conflict and the names of those who fought and died are not forgotten.

▲ **Source A** *The Menin Gate at Midnight* by the Australian artist William Longstaff. It was painted in 1927 after Longstaff witnessed the unveiling of the Menin Gate memorial in that year. The Menin Gate was built to commemorate the British and Empire soldiers who fought around Ypres in Belgium. The monument remembers the names of almost 55,000 soldiers who have no known grave because their bodies were never found. Their names are carved into the stone of the Gate. Longstaff himself fought in the First World War. He was injured at Gallipoli but went on to serve in France and Egypt. The painting shows ghostly soldiers marching across the fields in front of the Menin Gate.

## ACTIVITY

1. Study Source B. Who is Sassoon's poem aimed at? What message is he trying to convey to them?
2. Look at Source A. Why do you think Longstaff chose to present the Menin Gate in this way?
3. Which has more impact on you personally? An image about the cost of the War: the paintings (Sources A and F) or the photograph (Source C)? Explain your answer.

### Reconciliation

When you are standing at your hero's grave,

Or near some homeless village where he died,

Remember, through your heart's rekindling pride,

The German soldiers who were loyal and brave.

Men fought like brutes; and hideous things were done;

And you have nourished hatred harsh and blind.

But in that Golgotha perhaps you'll find

The mothers of the men who killed your son.

**Source B** 'Reconciliation' by Siegfried Sassoon (an officer on the Western Front). He wrote many poems about the War, including this one written in November 1918.

▼ **Source C** Tyne Cot Military Cemetery has the largest number of graves of any British Commonwealth war cemetery in the world. Nearly 12,000 British and Empire soldiers are buried there. Nearly 8,000 of the bodies were unidentifiable. These headstones are marked 'A Soldier of the Great War. Known unto God'.